APPLIQUÉ MADE EASY

Oxmoor House®

Contents

Workshop	4
Indian Summer	12
Whig Rose	15
Cherry	20
Tulip Garden	22
Irish Apple	27
Williamsburg Palm	30
My Daisy	35
Tulips	38
Calico Scallops	41
Grapevine	46

APPLIQUÉ MADE EASY

©1994 by Oxmoor House, Inc.

Book Division of Southern Progress Corporation
P.O. Box 2463, Birmingham, AL 35201

Published by Oxmoor House, Inc., and Leisure Arts, Inc.

All rights reserved. No part of this book may be reproduced in any form or by any means without the prior written permission of the publisher, excepting brief quotations in connection with reviews written specifically for inclusion in magazines or newspapers.

Library of Congress Catalog Number: 94-69237
ISBN: 0-8487-1261-7

Manufactured in the United States of America
First Printing 1994

Editor-in-Chief: Nancy J. Fitzpatrick
Editorial Director, Special Interest Publications: Ann H. Harvey
Senior Crafts Editor: Susan Ramey Wright
Senior Editor, Editorial Services: Olivia Kindig Wells
Art Director: James Boone

APPLIQUÉ MADE EASY

Editor: Carol Logan Newbill
Editorial Assistant: Janica Lynn York
Copy Editor: Jennifer K. Mathews
Production and Distribution Manager: Phillip Lee
Production Manager: Gail H. Morris
Associate Production Manager: Theresa L. Beste
Production Assistant: Marianne Jordan
Design Concept: Larry Hunter
Design Layout/Illustrations: Carol Loria
Patterns and Illustrations: Kelly Davis
Publishing Systems Administrator: Rick Tucker
Senior Photographer: John O'Hagan
Photostylist: Katie Stoddard

Dear Quilting Friends,

Say "appliqué" to a room full of seasoned quilters and watch how many of them run for cover. But those same quilters might not bat an eye at a complex pieced star design in which many points must intersect with precision.

What makes so many people *wrongly* assume that appliqué is a difficult technique? Perhaps some nebulous notion of perfection was instilled in them as children by mothers and teachers who admonished them to "stay in the lines" when they were coloring. Perhaps they think appliqué is like stay-in-the-lines coloring—it's hard and it's no fun.

But appliqué is easy—and it's fun! In appliqué, not only is perfection a needless concept, exactness and precision aren't crucial as in pieced quilts, where every point is supposed to be sharp and every corner is expected to match. If your appliquéd leaf turns out a little smaller, a little larger, or of a somewhat different shape than the one in the photograph, so much the better! In nature, no two leaves are ever the same.

True, quilts like Ami Simms's *Whig Rose* on page 15 and Penelope Wortman's *Tulips* on page 38 weren't made in a day. Traditional hand appliqué is hardly quick. If you like hand work but would like to speed up the process a little, try the freezer-paper technique. But if you want a method that's really quick and easy, maybe fusible webbing and machine stitching are right for you. Combine these with some quick-piecing ideas, such as the ones Gloria Brown used in *Irish Apple*, page 27, and you can finish an appliquéd masterpiece in record time. (A discussion of appliqué techniques begins on page 7.)

If you're new to appliqué, you might want to start with one of the simpler designs in this book, such as *Indian Summer* (page 12), *Irish Apple* (page 27), *My Daisy* (page 35), or *Calico Scallops* (page 41). You can make any of these quilts using either traditional hand appliqué or the speedier techniques of fusing and machine stitching. Chances are, once you see how easy appliqué really is, you'll be hooked on this fun form of needlework.

Happy stitching,

Susan R. Wright

WORKSHOP

Selecting Fabrics

The best fabric for quilts is 100% cotton. Yardage requirements are based on 44"-wide fabric and allow for shrinkage. All fabrics, including backing, should be machine-washed, dried, and pressed before cutting. Use warm water and detergent but not fabric softener.

Necessary Notions

- Scissors
- Rotary cutter and mat
- Acrylic rulers
- Template plastic
- Pencils for marking cutting lines
- Sewing needles
- Sewing thread
- Sewing machine
- Seam ripper
- Pins
- Iron and ironing board
- Quilting needles
- Thimble
- Hand quilting thread
- Machine quilting thread

Making Templates

A template is a duplication of a printed pattern, made from a sturdy material, which is traced onto fabric. Many regular shapes such as squares and triangles can be marked directly on the fabric with a ruler, but you need templates for other shapes. Some quiltmakers use templates for all shapes.

You can trace patterns directly onto template plastic. Or make a template by tracing a pattern onto graph paper and gluing the paper to posterboard or sandpaper. (Sandpaper will not slip on fabric.)

When a large pattern is given in two pieces, make one template for the complete piece.

Cut out the template on the marked line. It is important that a template be traced, marked, and cut accurately. If desired, punch out corner dots with a ⅛"-diameter hole punch **(Diagram 1)**.

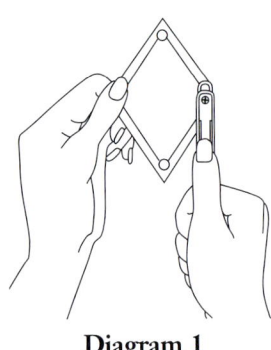

Diagram 1

Mark each template with its letter and grain line. Verify the template's accuracy, placing it over the printed pattern. Any discrepancy, however small, is multiplied many times as the quilt is assembled. Another way to check templates' accuracy is to make a test block before cutting more pieces.

Tracing Templates on Fabric

For hand piecing, templates should be cut to the finished size of the piece so seam lines can be marked on the fabric. Avoiding the selvage, place the template *facedown* on the *wrong* side of the fabric, aligning the template grain line with the straight grain. Hold the template firmly and trace around it. Repeat as needed, leaving ½" between tracings **(Diagram 2)**.

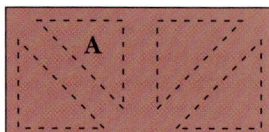

Diagram 2

For machine piecing, templates should include seam allowances. These templates are used in the same manner as for hand piecing, but you can mark the fabric using common lines for efficient cutting **(Diagram 3)**. Mark corners on fabric through holes in the template.

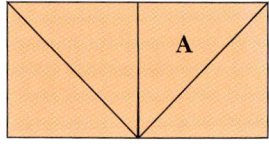

Diagram 3

For hand or machine piecing, use window templates to enhance accuracy by drawing and cutting out both cutting and sewing lines. The guidance of a drawn seam line is very useful for sewing set-in seams, when pivoting at a precise point is critical. Used on the right side of the fabric, window templates help you cut specific motifs with accuracy **(Diagram 4)**.

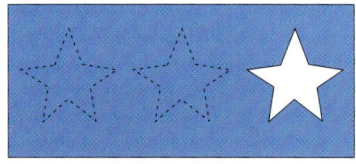

Diagram 4

For hand appliqué, templates should be made the finished size. Place templates *faceup* on the *right* side of the fabric. Position tracings at least ½" apart **(Diagram 5)**. Add a ¼" seam allowance around pieces when cutting.

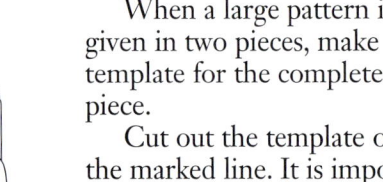

Diagram 5

Cutting

Grain Lines

Woven threads form the fabric's grain. Lengthwise grain, parallel to the selvages, has the least stretch; crosswise grain has a little more give.

Long strips such as borders should be cut lengthwise whenever possible and cut first to ensure that you have the necessary length. Usually, other pieces can be cut aligned with either grain.

Bias is the 45° diagonal line between the two grain directions. Bias has the most stretch and is used for curving strips such as flower stems. Bias is often preferred for binding.

Never use the selvage (finished edge). Selvage does not react to washing, drying, and pressing like the rest of the fabric and may pucker when the finished quilt is laundered.

Rotary Cutting

A rotary cutter, used with a protective mat and a ruler, takes getting used to but is very efficient for cutting strips, squares, and triangles. A rotary cutter is fast because you can measure and cut multiple layers with a single stroke, without templates or marking. It is also more accurate than cutting with scissors because fabrics remain flat and do not move during cutting.

Because the blade is very sharp, be sure to get a rotary cutter with a safety guard. Keep the guard in the safe position at all times, except when making a cut. *Always keep the cutter out of the reach of children.*

Use the cutter with a self-healing mat. A good mat for cutting strips is at least 23" wide.

1. Squaring the fabric is the first step in accurate cutting. Fold the fabric with selvages aligned. With the yardage to your right, align a small square ruler with the fold near the cut edge. Place a long ruler against the left side of the square **(Diagram 6).** Keeping the long ruler in place, remove the square. Hold the ruler in place with your left hand as you cut, rolling the cutter *away from you* along the ruler's edge with a steady motion. You can move your left hand along the ruler as you cut, but do not change the position of the ruler. *Keep your fingers away from the ruler's edge when cutting.*

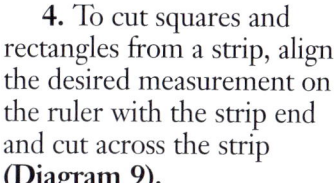

Diagram 6

2. Open the fabric. If the cut was not accurately perpendicular to the fold, the edge will be V-shaped instead of straight **(Diagram 7).** Correct the cut if necessary.

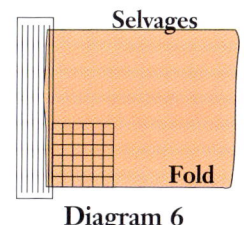

Diagram 7

3. With a transparent ruler, you can measure and cut at the same time. Fold the fabric in half again, aligning the selvages with the fold, making four layers that line up perfectly along the cut edge. Project instructions designate the strip width needed. Position the ruler to measure the correct distance from the edge **(Diagram 8)** and cut. The blade will easily cut through all four layers. Check the strip to be sure the cut is straight. The strip length is the width of the fabric, approximately 43" to 44". Using the ruler again, trim selvages, cutting about 3/8" from each end.

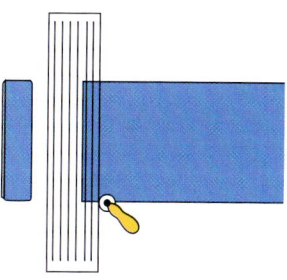

Diagram 8

4. To cut squares and rectangles from a strip, align the desired measurement on the ruler with the strip end and cut across the strip **(Diagram 9).**

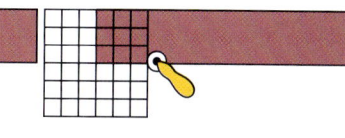

Diagram 9

5. Cut triangles from squares or rectangles. Cutting instructions often direct you to cut a square in half or in quarters diagonally to make right triangles, and this technique can apply to rectangles, too **(Diagram 10).** The outside edges of the square or rectangle are on the straight of the grain, so triangle sides cut on the diagonal are bias.

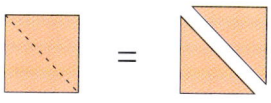
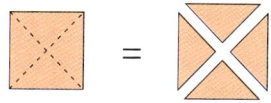
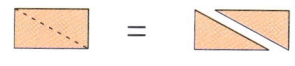

6. Some projects in this book use a time-saving technique called strip piecing. With this method, strips are joined to make a pieced band. Cut across the seams of this band to cut preassembled units **(Diagram 11).**

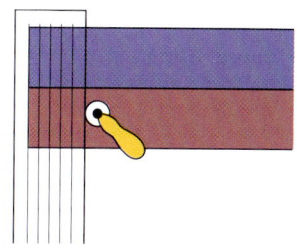

Diagram 11

Machine Piecing

Your sewing machine does not have to be a new, computerized model. A good straight stitch is all that's necessary, but it may be helpful to have a nice satin stitch for appliqué. Clean and oil your machine regularly, use good-quality thread, and replace needles frequently.

1. Patches for machine piecing are cut with the seam allowance included, but the sewing line is not usually marked. Therefore, a way to make a consistent ¼" seam is essential. Some presser feet have a right toe that is ¼" from the needle. Other machines have an adjustable needle that can be set for a ¼" seam. If your machine has neither feature, experiment to find how the fabric must be placed to make a ¼" seam. Mark this position on the presser foot or throat plate.

2. Use a stitch length that makes a strong seam but is not too difficult to remove with a seam ripper. The best setting is usually 10 to 12 stitches per inch.

3. Pin only when really necessary. If a straight seam is less than 4" and does not have to match an adjoining seam, pinning is not necessary.

4. When intersecting seams must align **(Diagram 12)**, match the units with right sides facing and push a pin through both seams at the seam line. Turn the pinned unit to the right side to check the alignment; then pin securely. As you sew, remove each pin just before the needle reaches it.

Figure 1
Intersecting seams aligned

Figure 2
Intersecting seams not aligned

Diagram 12

5. Block assembly diagrams are used throughout this book to show how pieces should be joined. Make small units first; then join them in rows and continue joining rows to finish the block **(Diagram 13)**. Blocks are joined in the same manner to complete the quilt top.

Diagram 13

6. Chain piecing saves time. Stack pieces to be sewn in pairs, with right sides facing. Join the first pair as usual. At the end of the seam, do not backstitch, cut the thread, or lift the presser foot. Just feed in the next pair of pieces—the machine will make a few stitches between pieces before the needle strikes the second piece of fabric. Continue sewing in this way until all pairs are joined. Stack the chain of pieces until you are ready to clip them apart **(Diagram 14)**.

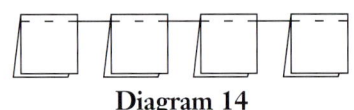
Diagram 14

7. Most seams are sewn straight across, from raw edge to raw edge. Since they will be crossed by other seams, they do not require backstitching to secure them.

8. When piecing diamonds or other angled seams, you may need to make set-in seams. For these, always mark the corner dots (shown on the patterns) on the fabric pieces. Stitch one side, starting at the outside edge and being careful not to sew beyond the dot into the seam allowance **(Diagram 15, Figure A)**. Backstitch. Align the other side of the piece as needed, with right sides facing. Sew from the dot to the outside edge **(Figure B)**.

9. Sewing curved seams requires extra care. First, mark the centers of both the convex (outward) and concave (inward) curves **(Diagram 16)**. Staystitch just inside the seam allowance of both pieces. Clip the concave piece to the stitching **(Figure A)**. With right sides facing and raw edges aligned, pin the two patches together at the center **(Figure B)** and at the left edge **(Figure C)**. Sew from edge to center, stopping frequently to check that the raw edges are aligned. Stop at the center with the needle down. Raise the presser foot and pin the pieces together from the center to the right edge. Lower the foot and continue to sew. Press seam allowances toward the concave curve **(Figure D)**.

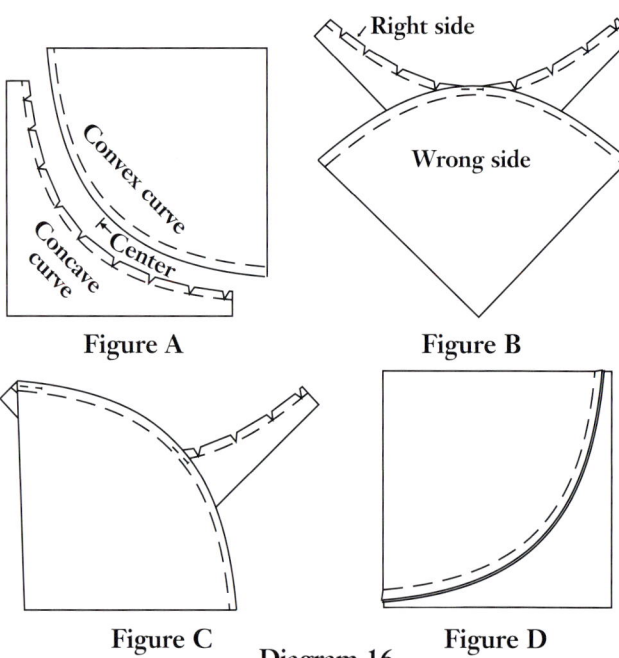
Figure A   Figure B
Figure C   Figure D
Diagram 16

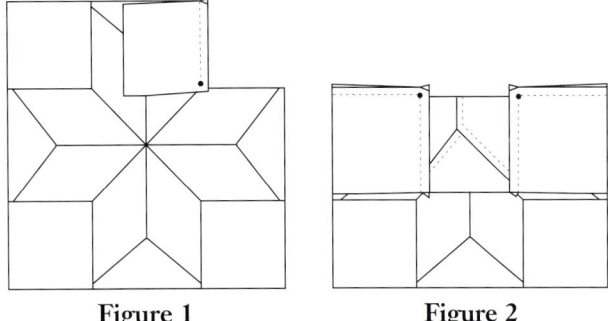
Figure 1   Figure 2
Diagram 15

Hand Piecing

Make a running stitch of 8 to 10 stitches per inch along the marked seam line on the wrong side of the fabric. Don't pull the fabric as you sew; let the pieces lie relaxed in your hand. Sew from seam line to seam line, not from edge to edge as in machine piecing.

When ending a line of stitching, backstitch over the last stitch and make a loop knot **(Diagram 17)**.

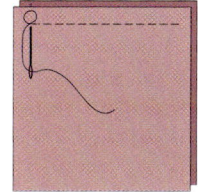
Diagram 17

Match seams and points accurately, pinning patches together before piecing. Align match points as described in Step 4 under Machine Piecing.

When joining units where several seams meet, do not sew over seam allowances; sew *through* them at the match point **(Diagram 18)**. When four or more seams meet, press the seam allowances in the same direction to reduce bulk **(Diagram 19)**.

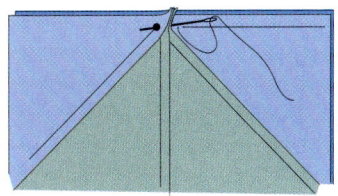 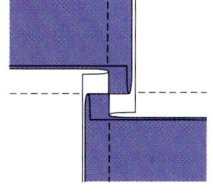

Diagram 18   **Diagram 19**

Pressing

Careful pressing is necessary for precise piecing. Press each seam as you go. Sliding the iron back and forth may push the seam out of shape. Use an up-and-down motion, lifting the iron from spot to spot. Press the seam flat on the wrong side. Open the piece and, on the right side, press both seam allowances to one side (usually toward the darker fabric). Pressing the seam open leaves tiny gaps through which batting may beard.

Appliqué

Traditional Hand Appliqué

Hand appliqué requires that you turn under a seam allowance around the shape to prevent frayed edges.

1. Trace around the template on the right side of the fabric. This line indicates where to turn the seam allowance. Cut each piece approximately ¼" outside the line.

2. For simple shapes, turn the edges by pressing the seam allowance to the back; complex shapes may require basting the seam allowance. Sharp points and strong curves are best appliquéd with freezer paper. Clip curves to make a smooth edge. With practice, you can work without pressing seam allowances, turning edges under with the needle as you sew.

3. Do not turn under any seam allowance that will be covered by another appliqué piece.

4. To stitch, use one strand of cotton-wrapped polyester sewing thread in a color that matches the appliqué. Use a slipstitch, but keep the stitch very small on the surface. Working from right to left (or left to right if you're left-handed), pull the needle through the base fabric and catch only a few threads on the folded edge of the appliqué. Reinsert the needle into the base fabric, under the top thread on the appliqué edge to keep the thread from tangling **(Diagram 20)**.

5. An alternative to slipstitching is to work a decorative buttonhole stitch around each figure **(Diagram 21)**.

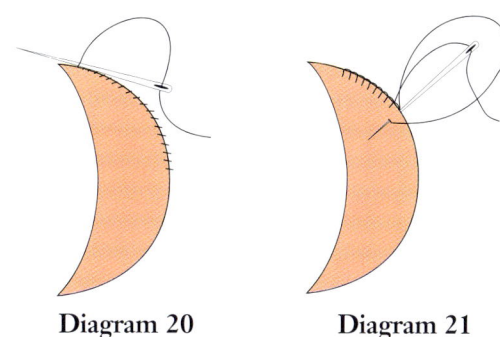

Diagram 20   **Diagram 21**

Freezer Paper Hand Appliqué

Supermarket freezer paper saves time because it eliminates the need for basting seam allowances.

1. Trace the template onto the *dull* side of the freezer paper and cut the paper on the marked line. *Note:* If a design is not symmetrical, turn the template over and trace a mirror image so the fabric piece won't be reversed when you cut it out.

2. Pin the freezer-paper shape, with its *shiny side* up, to the *wrong side* of the fabric. Following the paper shape and adding a scant ¼" seam allowance, cut out the fabric piece. Do not remove pins.

3. Using just the tip of a dry iron, press the seam allowance to the shiny side of the paper. Be careful not to touch the freezer paper with the iron.

4. Appliqué the piece to the background as in traditional appliqué. Trim the fabric from behind the shape, leaving ¼" seam allowances. Separate the freezer paper from the fabric with your fingernail and pull gently to remove it. If you prefer not to trim the background fabric, pull out the freezer paper before you complete stitching.

5. Sharp points require special attention. Turn the point down and press it **(Diagram 22, Figure A)**. Fold the seam allowance on one side over the point and press **(Figure B)**; then fold the other seam allowance over the point and press **(Figure C)**.

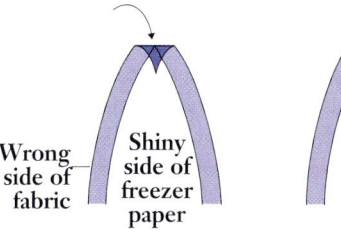 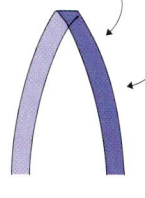

Wrong side of fabric   Shiny side of freezer paper

Figure A   **Figure B**   **Figure C**

Diagram 22

6. When pressing curved edges, clip sharp inward curves **(Diagram 23)**. If the shape doesn't curve smoothly, separate the paper from the fabric with your fingernail and try again.

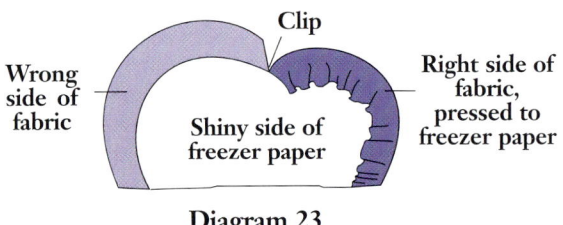

Diagram 23

Diagram 25

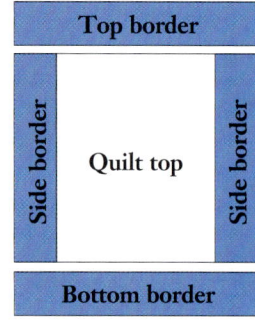

Diagram 26

7. Remove the pins when all seam allowances have been pressed to the freezer paper. Position the prepared appliqué right side up on the background fabric. Press to adhere it to the background fabric.

Machine Appliqué

A machine-sewn satin stitch makes a neat edging. For machine appliqué, cut appliqué pieces without adding seam allowances.

Using fusible web to adhere pieces to the background adds a stiff extra layer to the appliqué and is not appropriate for some quilts. It is best used on small pieces, difficult fabrics, or for wall hangings and accessories in which added stiffness is acceptable. The web prevents fraying and shifting during appliqué.

Place tear-away stabilizer under the background fabric behind the appliqué. Machine-stitch the appliqué edges with a satin stitch or close-spaced zigzag **(Diagram 24)**. Test the stitch length and width on a sample first. Use an open-toed presser foot. Remove the stabilizer when appliqué is complete.

Diagram 24

Measuring Borders

Because seams may vary and fabrics may stretch a bit, opposite sides of your assembled quilt top may not be the same measurement. You can (and should) correct this when you add borders.

Measure the length of each side of the quilt. Trim the side border strips to match the *shorter* of the two sides. Join borders to the quilt as described below, easing the longer side of the quilt to fit the border. Join borders to the top and bottom edges in the same manner.

Straight Borders

Side borders are usually added first **(Diagram 25)**. With right sides facing and raw edges aligned, pin the center of one border strip to the center of one side of the quilt top. Pin the border to the quilt at each end and then pin along the side as desired. Machine-stitch with the border strip on top. Press the seam allowance toward the border. Trim excess border fabric at each end. In the same manner, add the border to the opposite side and then the top and bottom borders **(Diagram 26)**.

Mitered Borders

1. Measure your quilt sides. Trim the side border strips to fit the shorter side *plus* the width of the border *plus* 2".

2. Center the measurement of the shorter side on one border strip, placing a pin at each end and at the center of the measurement.

3. With right sides facing and raw edges aligned, match the pins on the border strip to the center and corners of the longer side of the quilt. (Border fabric will extend beyond the corners.)

4. Start machine-stitching at the top pin, backstitching to lock the stitches. Continue to sew, easing the quilt between pins. Stop at the last pin and backstitch. Join remaining borders in the same manner. Press seam allowances toward borders.

5. With right sides facing, fold the quilt diagonally, aligning the raw edges of adjacent borders. Pin securely **(Diagram 27)**.

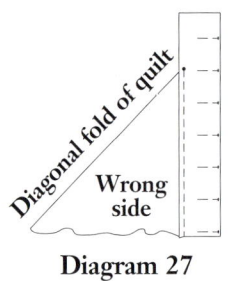

Diagram 27

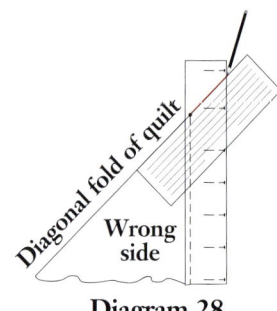

Diagram 28

6. Align a yardstick or quilter's ruler along the diagonal fold **(Diagram 28)**. Holding the ruler firmly, mark a line from the end of the border seam to the raw edge.

7. Start machine-stitching at the beginning of the marked line, backstitch, and then stitch on the line out to the raw edge.

8. Unfold the quilt to be sure that the corner lies flat. Correct the stitching if necessary. Trim the seam allowance to ¼".

9. Miter the remaining corners in the same manner. Press the corner seams open.

Quilting Without Marking

Some quilts can be quilted in-the-ditch (right along the seam line), outline-quilted (¼" from the seam line), or echo-quilted (lines of quilting rippling outward from the design like waves on a pond). These methods can be used without any marking at all. If you are machine quilting, simply use the edge of your presser foot and the seam line as a guide. If you are hand quilting, by the time you have pieced a quilt top, your eye will be practiced enough for you to produce straight, even quilting without the guidance of marked lines.

Marking Quilting Designs

Many quilters like to mark the entire top at one time, a practice that requires long-lasting markings. The most common tool for this purpose is a sharp **pencil.** However, most pencils are made with an oil-based graphite lead, which often will not wash out completely. Look for a high-quality artist's pencil marked "2H" or higher (the higher the number, the harder the lead, and the lighter the line it will make). Sharpen the pencil frequently to keep the line on the fabric thin and light. Or try a mechanical pencil with a 0.5-mm lead. It will maintain a fine line without sharpening.

While you are in the art supply store, get a **white plastic eraser** (brand name Magic Rub). This eraser, used by professional drafters and artists, will cleanly remove the carbon smudges left by pencil lead without fraying the fabric or leaving eraser crumbs.

Water- and **air-soluble marking pens** are convenient, but controversial, marking tools. Some quilters have found that the marks reappear, often up to several years later, while others have no problems with them.

Be sure to test these pens on each fabric you plan to mark and *follow package directions exactly.* Because the inks can be permanently set by heat, be very careful with a marked quilt. Do not leave it in your car on a hot day and never touch it with an iron until the marks have been removed. Plan to complete the quilting within a year after marking it with a water-soluble pen.

Air-soluble pens are best for marking small sections at a time. The marks disappear within 24 to 48 hours, but the ink remains in the fabric until it is washed. After the quilt is completed and before it is used, rinse it twice in clear, cool water, using no soap, detergent, or bleach. Let the quilt air-dry.

For dark fabrics, the cleanest marker you can use is a thin sliver of pure, white **soap.** Choose a soap that contains no creams, deodorants, dyes, or perfumes; these added ingredients may leave a residue on the fabric.

Other marking tools include **colored pencils** made specifically for marking fabric and **tailor's chalk** (available in powdered, stick, and traditional cake form). When using chalk, mark small sections of the quilt at a time because the chalk rubs off easily.

Quilting Stencils

Quilting patterns can be purchased as precut stencils. Simply lay these on your quilt top and mark the design through the cutout areas.

To make your own stencil of a printed quilting pattern, such as the one below, use a permanent marker to trace the design onto a blank sheet of template plastic. Then use a craft knife to cut out the design.

Quilting Stencil Pattern

Making a Quilt Backing

Some fabric and quilt shops sell 90" and 108" widths of 100% cotton fabric that are very practical for quilt backing. However, the instructions in this book always give backing yardage based on 44"-wide fabric.

When using 44"-wide fabric, all quilts wider than 41" will require a pieced backing. For quilts 41" to 80" wide, you will need an amount of fabric equal to two times the desired *length* of the unfinished backing. (The unfinished backing should be at least 3" larger on all sides than the quilt top.)

The simplest method of making a backing is to cut the fabric in half widthwise **(Diagram 29),** and then sew the two panels together lengthwise. This results in a backing with a vertical center seam. Press the seam allowances to one side.

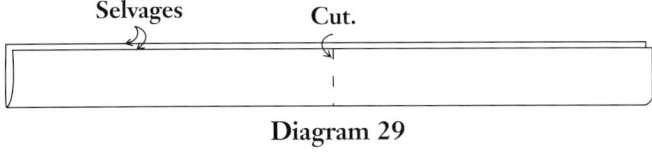

Diagram 29

Another method of seaming the backing results in two vertical seams and a center panel of fabric. This method is often preferred by quilt show judges. Begin by cutting the fabric in half widthwise. Open the two lengths and stack them, with right sides facing and selvages aligned. Stitch along *both* selvage edges to create a tube of fabric **(Diagram 30).** Cut down the center of the top layer of fabric only and open the fabric flat **(Diagram 31).** Press seam allowances to one side.

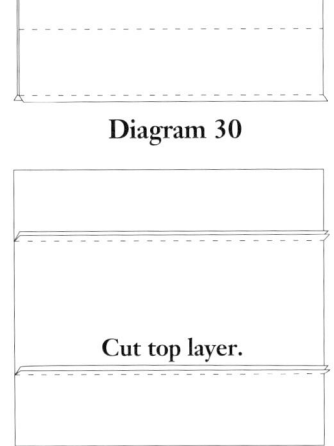

Diagram 30

Diagram 31

If the quilt is wider than 80", it is more economical to cut the fabric into three lengths that are the desired width of the backing. Join the three lengths so that the seams are horizontal to the quilt, rather than vertical. For this method, you'll need an amount of fabric equal to three times the *width* of the unfinished backing.

Fabric requirements in this book reflect the most economical method of seaming the backing fabric.

Layering and Basting

After the quilt top and backing are made, the next steps are layering and basting in preparation for quilting.

Prepare a large working surface to spread out the quilt—a large table, two tables pushed together, or the floor. Place the backing on the working surface wrong side up. Unfold the batting and place it on top of the backing, smoothing away any wrinkles or lumps.

Lay the quilt top wrong side down on top of the batting and backing. Make sure the edges of the backing and quilt top are parallel.

Knot a long strand of sewing thread and use a long (darning) needle for basting. Begin basting in the center of the quilt and baste out toward the edges. The basting stitches should cover an ample amount of the quilt so that the layers do not shift during quilting.

Machine quilters use nickel-plated safety pins for basting so there will be no basting threads to get caught on the presser foot. Safety pins, spaced approximately 4" apart, can be used by hand quilters, too.

Hand Quilting

Hand-quilted stitches should be evenly spaced, with the spaces between stitches about the same length as the stitches themselves. The *number* of stitches per inch is less important than the *uniformity* of the stitching. Don't worry if you take only five or six stitches per inch; just be consistent throughout the project.

Machine Quilting

For machine quilting, the backing and batting should be 3" larger all around than the quilt top, because the quilting process pushes the quilt top fabric outward. After quilting, trim the backing and batting to the same size as the quilt top.

Thread your bobbin with good-quality sewing thread (not quilting thread) in a color to match the backing. Use a top thread color to match the quilt top or use invisible nylon thread.

An even-feed or walking foot will feed all the quilt's layers through the machine at the same speed. It is possible to machine-quilt without this foot (by experimenting with tension and presser foot pressure), but it will be much easier *with* it. If you do not have this foot, get one from your sewing machine dealer.

Straight-Grain Binding

1. Mark the fabric in horizontal lines the width of the binding **(Diagram 32)**.

A	↕ width of binding	
B		A
C		B
D		C
E		D
F		E
		F

Diagram 32

2. With right sides facing, fold the fabric in half, offsetting drawn lines by matching letters and raw edges **(Diagram 33)**. Stitch a ¼" seam.

3. Cut the binding in a continuous strip, starting with one end and following the marked lines around the tube. Press the strip in half lengthwise.

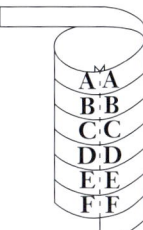

Diagram 33

Continuous Bias Binding

This technique can be used to make continuous bias for appliqué as well as for binding.

1. Cut a square of fabric in half diagonally to form two triangles. With right sides facing, join the triangles **(Diagram 34)**. Press the seam allowance open.

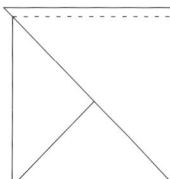

Diagram 34

2. Mark parallel lines the desired width of the binding **(Diagram 35)**, taking care not to stretch the bias. With right sides facing, align the raw edges (indicated as Seam 2). As you align the edges, offset one Seam 2 point past its natural matching point by one line. Stitch the seam; then press the seam allowance open.

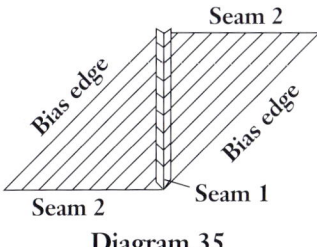

Diagram 35

3. Cut the binding in a continuous strip, starting with the protruding point and following the marked lines around the tube **(Diagram 36)**. Press the strip in half lengthwise.

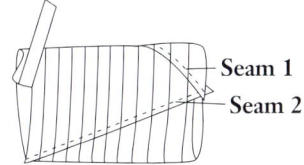

Diagram 36

Applying Binding

Binding is applied to the front of the quilt first. You may begin anywhere on the edge of the quilt except at the corner.

1. Matching raw edges, lay the binding on the quilt. Fold down the top corner of the binding at a 45° angle, align the raw edges, and pin **(Diagram 37)**.

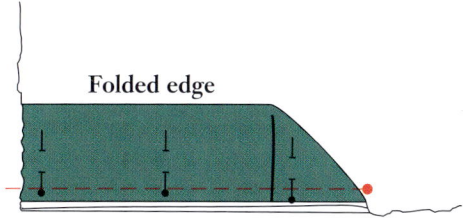

Diagram 37

2. Beginning at the folded end, machine-stitch the binding to the quilt. Stop stitching ¼" from the corner and backstitch. Fold the binding strip diagonally away from the quilt, making a 45° angle **(Diagram 38)**.

3. Fold the binding strip straight down along the next side to be stitched, creating a pleat in the corner. Position the needle at the ¼" seam line of the new side **(Diagram 39)**. Make a few stitches, backstitch, and then stitch the seam. Continue until all corners and sides are done. Overlap the end of the binding strip over the beginning fold and stitch about 2" beyond it. Trim any excess binding.

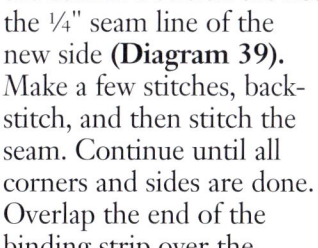

Diagram 38

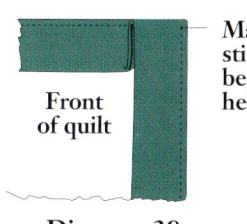

Diagram 39

4. Turn the binding over the raw edge of the quilt. Slipstitch it in place on the back, using thread that matches the binding. The fold at the beginning of the binding strip will create a neat, angled edge when it is folded to the back.

5. At each corner, fold the binding to form a miter **(Diagram 40)**. Hand-stitch the miters closed if desired.

Diagram 40

Indian Summer

Don't look for exact duplicates of the prints that Oxmoor House Senior Crafts Editor Susan Ramey Wright used in her quilted interpretation of a shower of autumn leaves. Susan bought the fabrics and began this quilt in 1980. Over the years, she brought out the autumn leaf project occasionally, but put it away as other quilt ideas were born.

"Each year, sometime in late summer, I'd get nostalgic for October and stitch a few more autumn leaf blocks," says Susan. "But then as Christmas got closer, I'd long to make something red and green, and I'd put the leaf quilt away again."

In the summer of 1991, Susan stitched the last of the blocks, framed them with a simple plaid sashing, and finished the project by echo quilting around each leaf. Now, when muggy August afternoons make her long for October evenings, she has her finished quilt to remind her that Indian Summer is just a couple of full moons away.

Quilt by Susan Ramey Wright,
Leeds, Alabama

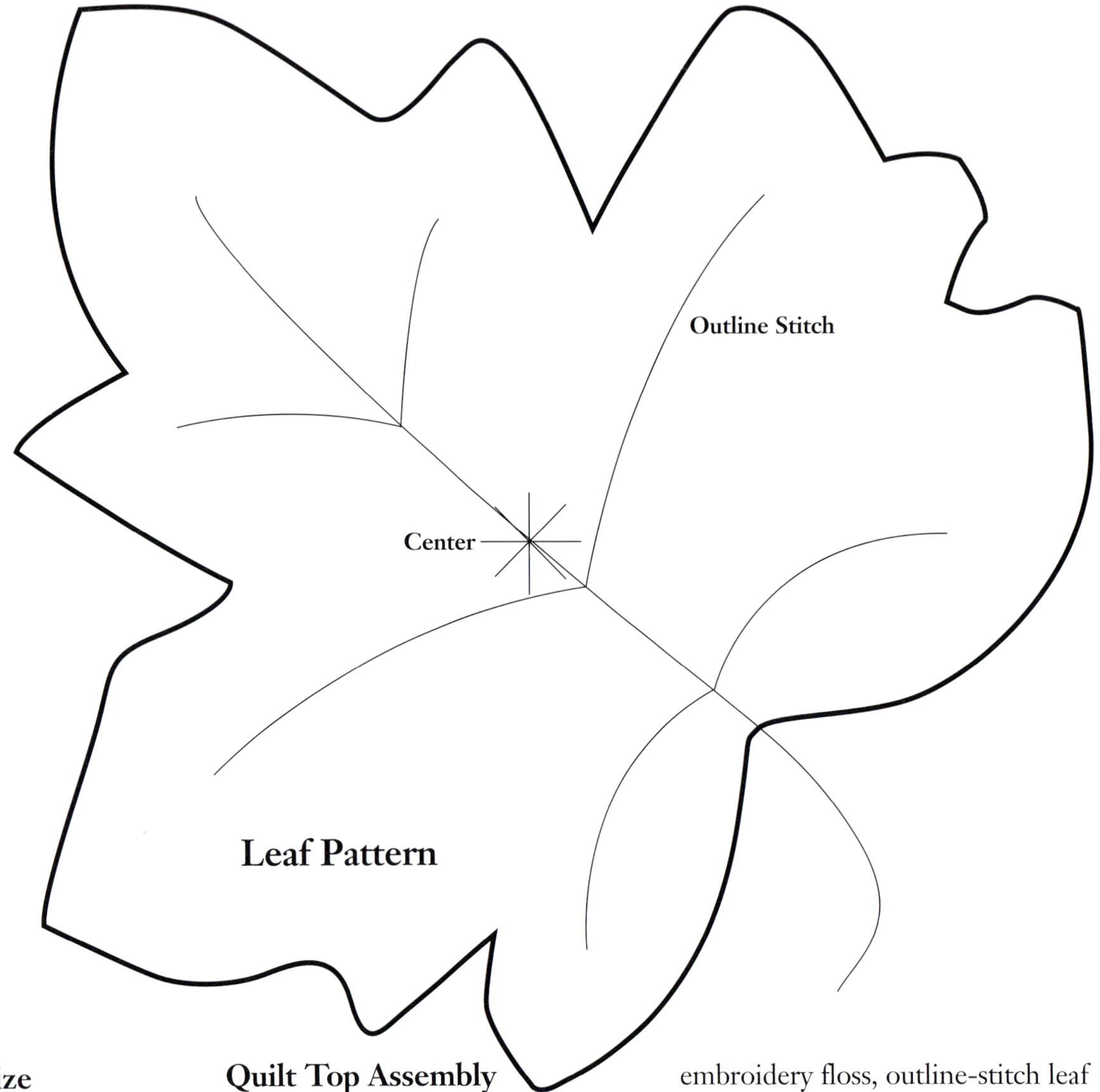

Leaf Pattern

Outline Stitch

Center

Finished Quilt Size
77½" x 87"

Number of Blocks and Finished Size
72 blocks   8" x 8"

Fabric Requirements
Muslin   4½ yards*
Brown plaid   2 yards
Brown solid   ⅜ yard
Assorted prints   Scraps**
Backing   5¼ yards
Black embroidery floss

*Includes fabric for straight-grain binding.

**Or 12 (¼-yard) pieces

Number to Cut
Leaf Pattern   72 assorted prints

Quilt Top Assembly

1. From muslin, cut 72 (8½") squares. Fold each square in half vertically, horizontally, and diagonally, finger-pressing folds to make appliqué placement guidelines.

From brown plaid, cut 161 (2" x 8½") sashing strips. From brown solid, cut 90 (2") sashing squares. Set sashing strips and squares aside.

2. Place each square over leaf pattern, matching center of fabric with marked center on pattern. Lightly trace leaf and stem outlines on muslin. Turn under seam allowances on leaf pieces. Pin in place on muslin, aligning edges with traced outlines. Appliqué leaves to make 72 blocks. Using 2 strands of embroidery floss, outline-stitch leaf veins and stems.

3. Referring to photograph and **Row Assembly Diagram**, join 8 blocks and 9 sashing strips to make 1 block row. Repeat to make 9 block rows.

4. Referring to **Row Assembly Diagram**, join 8 sashing strips and 9 sashing squares to make 1 sashing row. Repeat to make 10 sashing rows.

5. Join rows, alternating sashing rows and block rows.

Quilting
Outline-quilt leaves and sashing squares.

Finished Edges
Bind with straight-grain binding made from remaining muslin.

Block Row

Sashing Row

Row Assembly Diagram

Whig Rose

Quilt by Ami Simms, Flint, Michigan.

Special memories abound within this quilt for Ami Simms. "During the time I was working on *Whig Rose*, we applied to adopt a child, greeted our Korean daughter at the airport, and lost her maternal grandfather to cancer," remembers Ami.

She drafted the block design from a postcard of a 19th-century variation of the Whig Rose pattern and complemented it with a border of roses. Even though *Whig Rose* appears to use yards of bias strips, Ami recommends cutting stems and vines using templates.

Finished Quilt Size
79" x 79"

Number of Blocks and Finished Size
9 blocks   17" x 17"

Fabric Requirements
Red	⅝ yard
Red print	¾ yard
Navy	⅛ yard
Navy print	¾ yard
Green	4 yards
White	6 yards
Red for bias binding	1¼ yards
Backing	4⅝ yards

Number to Cut
Template A	28 red print
Template B	68 navy print
Template C	68 red
Template D	292 green
Template E	52 red
Template F	13 navy
Template G	20 green
Template H	20 green
Template I	20 green
Template J	12 green
Template J rev.*	12 green
Templates K, L, M	8 green vines**
Template N	4 green
Template N rev.*	4 green

*Flip or turn over template if fabric design is not reversible.

**Match ends of templates K, L, M for one complete vine. See Template Placement Diagram for One-piece Vine.

Quilt Top Assembly

1. Cut 9 (17½") squares from white. Finger-press each square diagonally; then finger-press again on the opposite diagonal to find center and to form guidelines for appliqué. Appliqué 5 squares with flowers and stems, as shown in **Block Placement Diagram.**

For remaining 4 squares, place 1 flower (B) with center (C) and 2 leaves (D) in each corner. Place flower petals (E) and circle (F) in center, as shown in quilt photograph, and appliqué.

2. Referring to quilt photograph for placement, join appliquéd squares in 3 rows of 3 squares

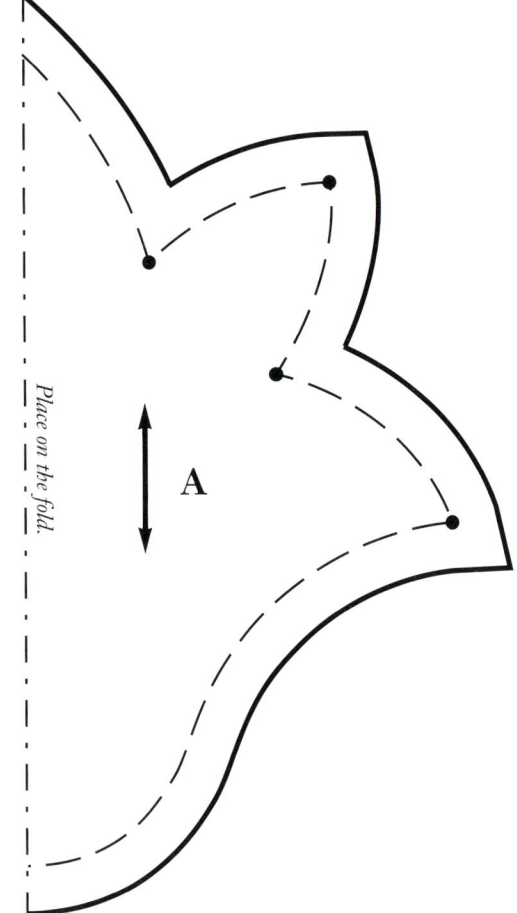

each. Join rows to complete center section.

3. Cut 4 border strips, 14½" wide, from white. Referring to **Border Placement Diagram,** pin vines and leaves in place and appliqué. Appliqué flowers. Join strips to center section and miter corners. Appliqué center piece (F) to corner flowers.

Block Placement Diagram

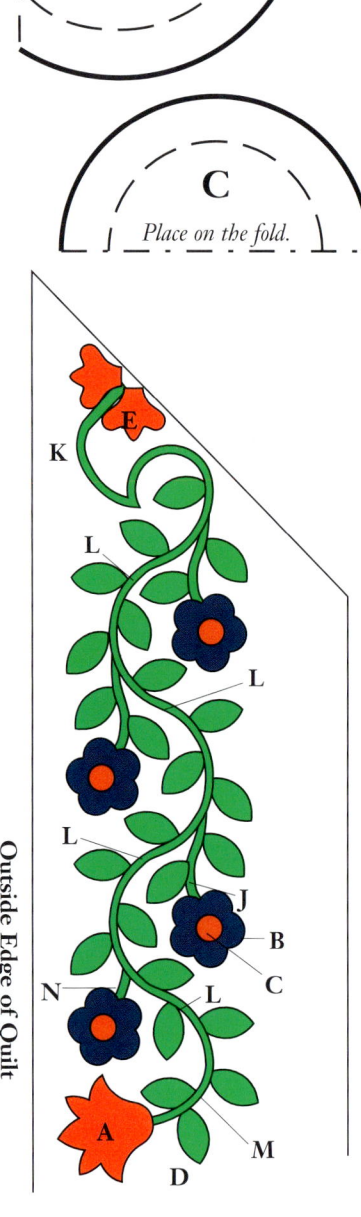

Border Placement Diagram

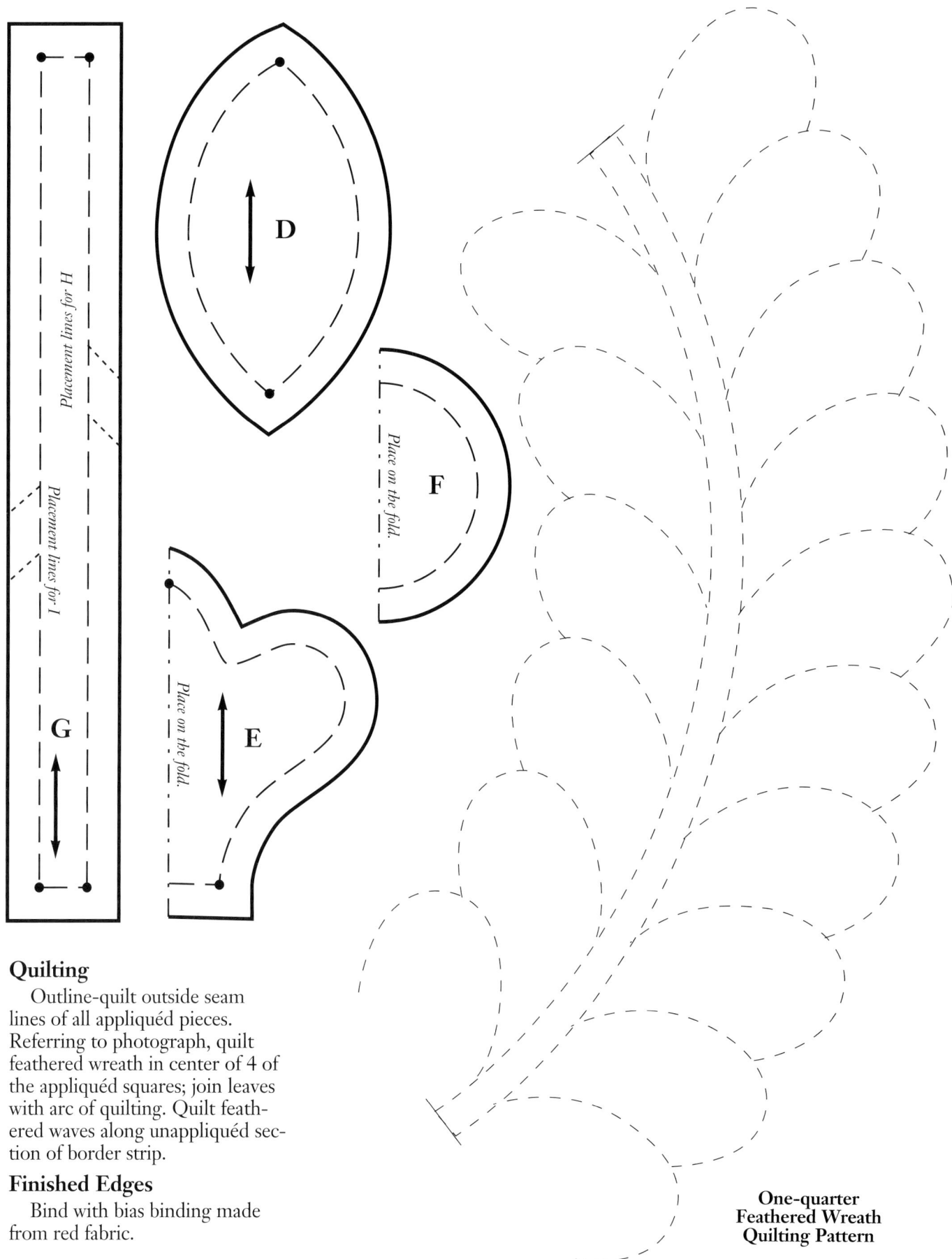

Quilting

Outline-quilt outside seam lines of all appliquéd pieces. Referring to photograph, quilt feathered wreath in center of 4 of the appliquéd squares; join leaves with arc of quilting. Quilt feathered waves along unappliquéd section of border strip.

Finished Edges

Bind with bias binding made from red fabric.

One-quarter Feathered Wreath Quilting Pattern

17

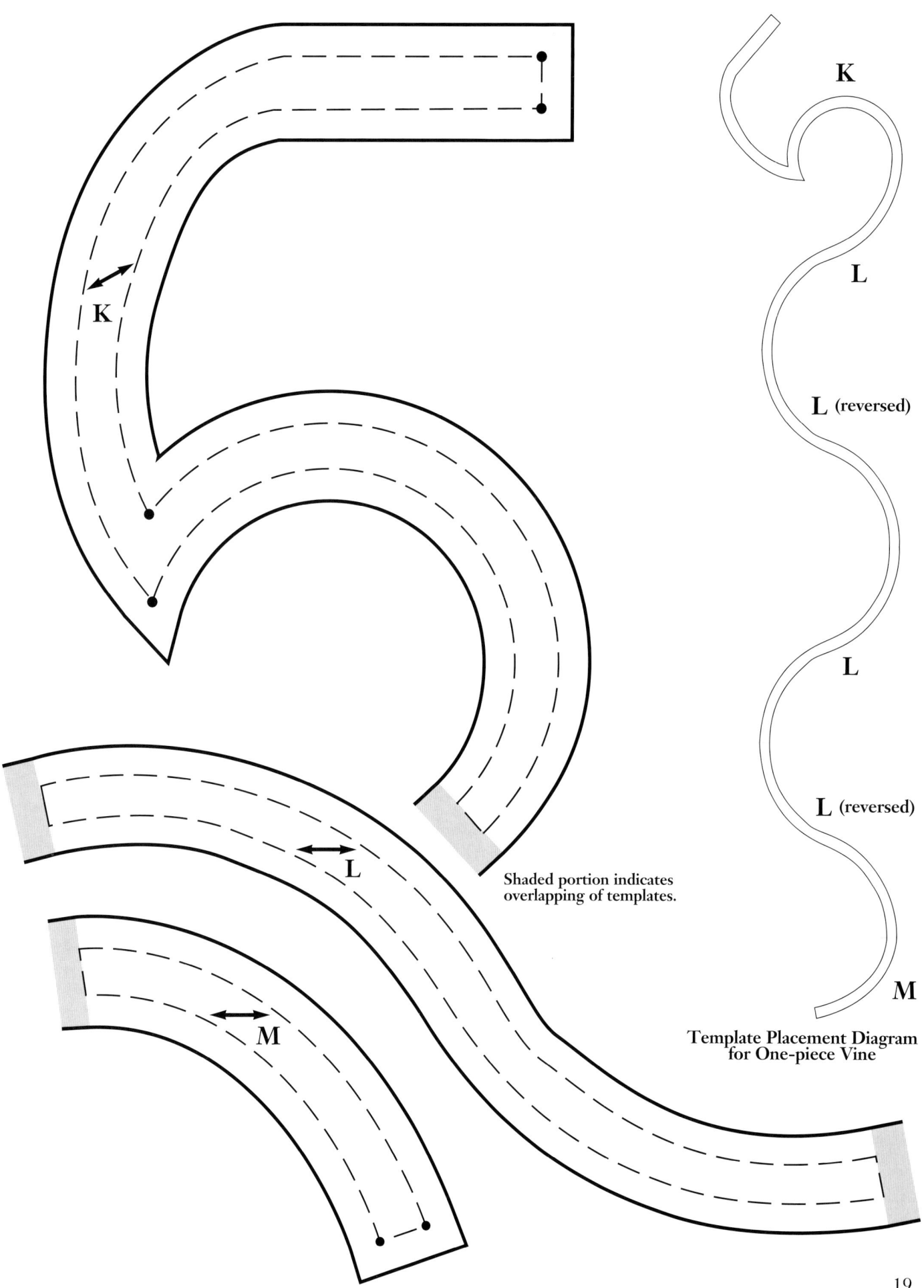

Cherry

*Quilt by Helen Louise Lindsey
Owned by David Sanders,
Mobile, Alabama*

Clusters of cherries, believed to be symbols for sweet character and good works, were popular motifs among appliqué quilters throughout the United States, especially during the original era of the Baltimore Album quilts. Cherries embellished floral wreaths, cornucopias, baskets, and other designs. Here clusters of them stand alone in a radiant splash of color and symmetry.

Helen Louise Lindsey's adeptness in fine needlework is represented in every cherry. Each is round, of equal size, and lies flat, and each cherry is evenly spaced in relation to the next one.

The rows and rows of cross-hatched quilting over this large quilt make it a noteworthy quilting feat. Oh, by the way, this is one of two identical quilts!

Finished Quilt Size
96" x 113"

Number of Blocks and Finished Size
20 blocks   17" x 17"

Fabric Requirements
Red   2 yards
Green   2½ yards
Muslin   9½ yards
Muslin for bias
   binding   1¼ yards
Backing   9¾ yards

Number to Cut
Template A   840 red
Template B   240 green
Template B rev.*   240 green
Template C   240 green

*Flip or turn over template if fabric design is not reversible.

Quilt Top Assembly

1. Cut 20 (17½") squares from muslin. Place cherries (A) and leaves (B) on squares, as shown in **Placement Diagram**, and appliqué. Note that the cherry placement leaves a space approximately 5" square in the center. Appliqué stems (C) as shown.

2. Join 4 blocks at sides to form a row. Make 5 rows. Join rows.

3. Cut 18 (14½" x 17½") rectangles from muslin. Cut 4 (14½") squares from muslin for corners. Appliqué with cherries, leaves, and stems, as shown in **Placement Diagram** and in quilt photograph.

4. Join 5 appliquéd rectangles at sides to form a border. Make 2. Refer to quilt photograph for border placement and join to sides of quilt.

5. Join 4 appliquéd rectangles each, as before, to form borders for top and bottom of quilt. Join an appliquéd square to each end. Join borders to top and bottom of quilt.

Quilting
Quilt background with 1" diagonal cross-hatching pattern.

Finished Edges
Bind with bias binding made from muslin.

Perfect Cherries

To make perfectly circular, ready-to-appliqué cherries, use a pressing template and a few gathering stitches.

From cardboard or other heat-resistant material, cut a circular template using pattern A *without* seam allowances.

Using a long running stitch, stitch by hand around the edges of one cherry (A), about ⅛" to ¼" from the raw edge. Center the cardboard template on the wrong side of the cherry and pull the thread to gather the stitches. Press. Loosen the gathering stitches enough to remove the template, and press again to flatten.

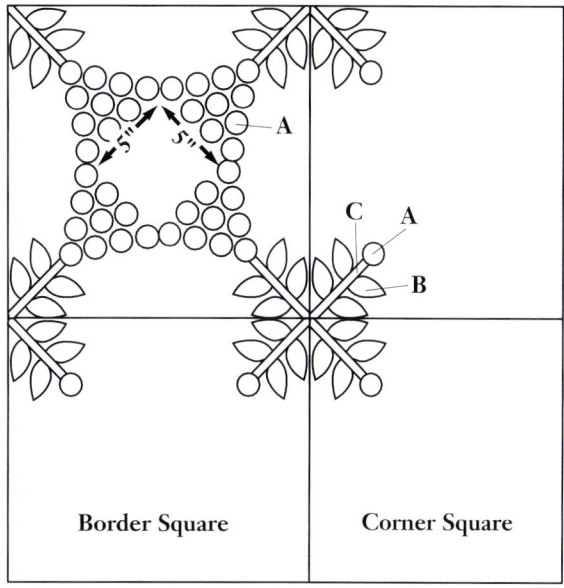

Placement Diagram

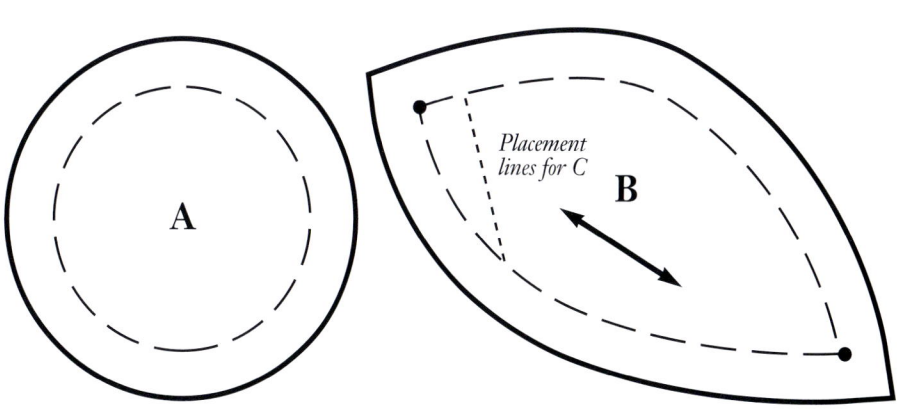

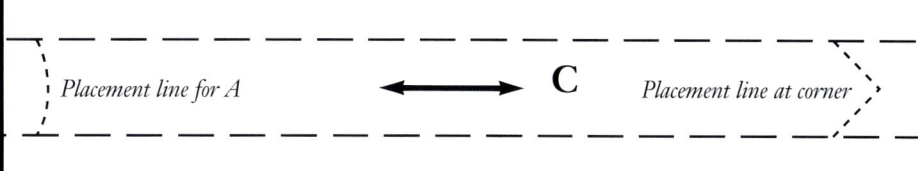

Tulip Garden

*Quilt by Hallie O'Kelley,
Tuscaloosa, Alabama*

Hallie O'Kelley's *Tulip Garden* uses flower designs, adapted from one of her original note cards and screen-printed onto solid fabric. By screen-printing, Hallie can get both the color and design she wants. "I use screen printing, not as a substitute for an appliquéd design, but rather to achieve fabric colors and designs that are my own and couldn't be achieved by using commercial fabrics," says Hallie.

Patterns and instructions in this book are given for appliquéd tulips. But if you'd rather try screen printing, use patterns without seam allowances and refer to one of the many instructional books available at your local library.

Finished Quilt Size
73" x 90"

Number of Blocks and Finished Size
15 blocks   16¼" x 12"

Fabric Requirements
Muslin*   6½ yards
Pink   1 yard
Dark rose   1¼ yards
Green   2½ yards
Backing   5¼ yards

*Includes fabric for bias binding.

Number to Cut
Template A   15 pink
Template B   30 pink
Template C   15 pink
Template D   15 dark rose
Template E   15 dark rose
Template F   15 dark rose
Template G   15 dark rose
Template H   15 dark rose
Template I   71 pink
               71 dark rose
               70 green
Template J   15 green
Template K   15 green
Template L   15 green
Template M   15 green
Template N   15 green
Template O   15 green
Template P   15 green
Template Q   15 green
Template R   15 green

Quilt Top Assembly

1. From muslin, cut 2 (6½" x 78½") strips for side borders and 2 (6½" x 73¼") strips for top and bottom borders. For sashing, cut 4 (3½" x 78½") and 18 (3½" x 16¾") strips from muslin. Set borders and sashing strips aside.

Also from muslin, cut 15 (16¾" x 12½") blocks. Fold each square in half vertically and horizontally, finger-pressing folds to make guidelines for placement of middle tulip.

2. To make 1 tulip block, appliqué 3 tulips and leaves to 1 muslin rectangle as shown in **Block Placement Diagram**. Repeat to make 15 blocks.

3. To make sashing, appliqué 6 tulips side by side to 1 (3½" x 16¾") muslin strip, alternating colors as shown in quilt photograph. Repeat to appliqué 18 strips.

To 1 (3½" x 78½") muslin strip, appliqué 26 tulips, alternating colors as shown in quilt photograph.

4. Join 5 blocks and 6 short sashing strips to form 1 vertical row. Repeat to make 3 rows. Join rows with long sashing strips as shown in photograph.

5. Join (6½" x 78½") border strips to sides of quilt. Join (6½" x 73½") border strips to top and bottom of quilt, butting corners.

Quilting
Quilt tulips as shown in **Quilting Diagram**. Outline-quilt sashing tulips. Quilt vertical lines midway between sashing tulips as shown in photograph. Quilt remainder in parallel horizontal lines 1" apart.

Finished Edges
Bind with bias binding made from muslin.

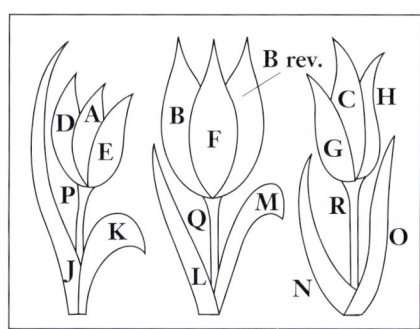

Block Placement Diagram

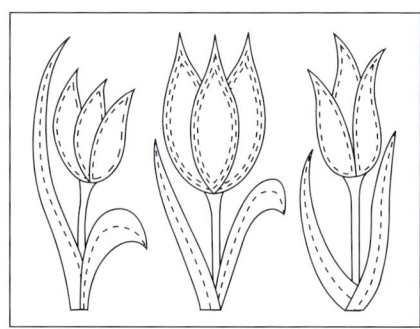

Quilting Diagram

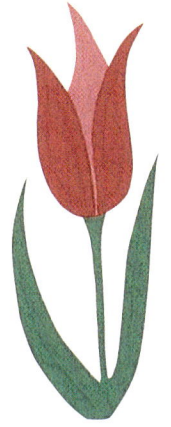

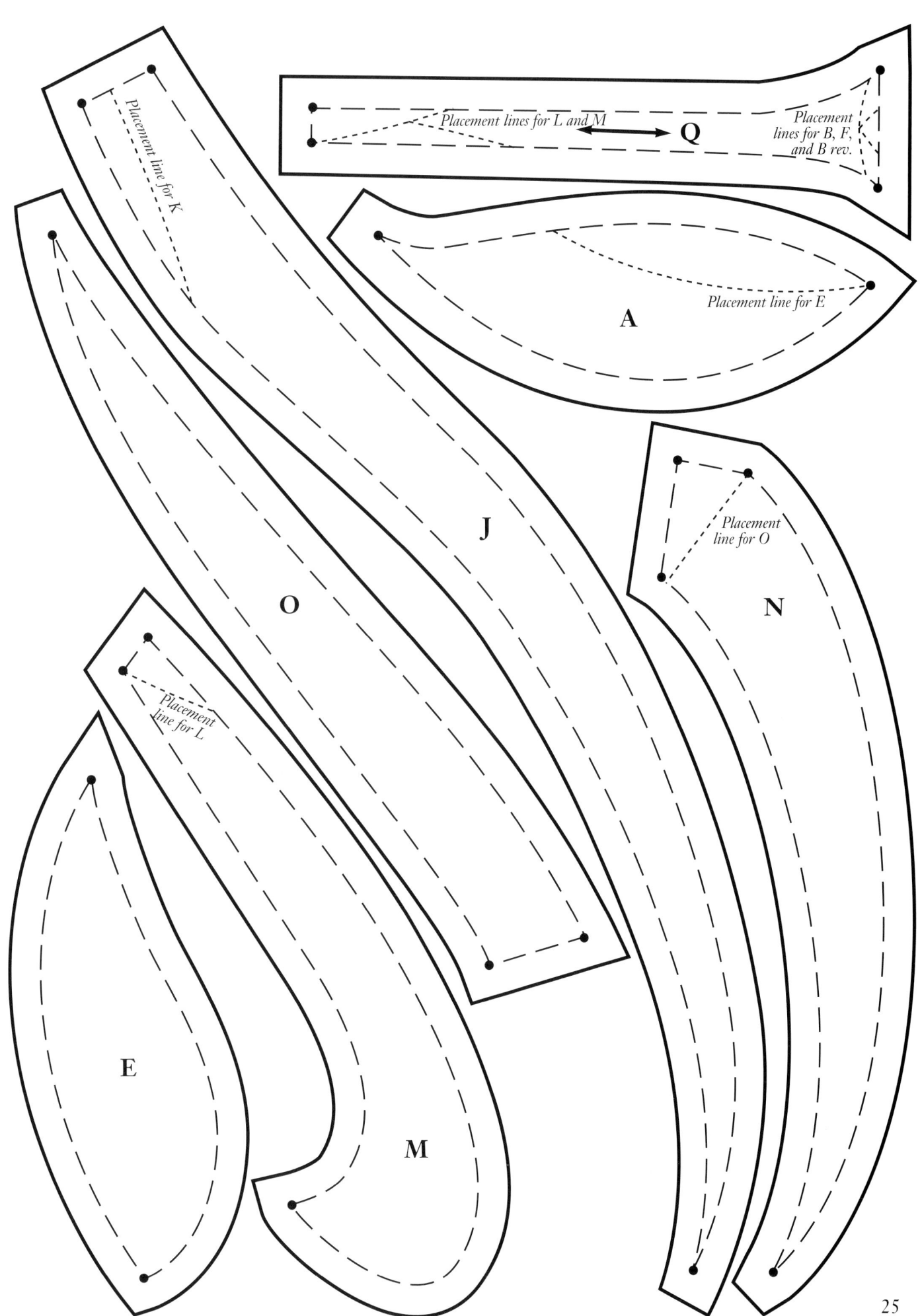

Irish Apple

*Quilt by Gloria Brown,
Tulsa, Oklahoma*

Mix 25 freshly picked, scrumptious red apples with a handsome Irish Chain, and you have the *Irish Apple*. Strip-pieced in hues of red, green, and blue, this quilt preserves the charm of the apple orchard for all to share.

And while you're busy appliquéing apples, don't be surprised if you have a sudden craving for a nibble of that crunchy fruit. Just look what happened to the apple in the lower right corner of Gloria's quilt.

Finished Quilt Size
78" x 78"

Number of Blocks and Finished Size
24 Apple blocks 10" x 10"
1 Apple Core block 10" x 10"
24 Irish Chain blocks 10" x 10"

Fabric Requirements
Red 2½ yards
Green 2¼ yards
Navy* 5¾ yards
Brown ⅛ yard
White 2¾ yards
Backing 4½ yards

*Includes fabric for bias binding.

Number to Cut
Template A 24 red
Template B 1 red
Template C 25 green
Template D 25 brown

Quilt Top Assembly

1. From white, cut 8 (6½"-wide) crosswise strips (selvage to selvage). Set aside.

From green, cut 2 (2½" x 74½") and 2 (2½" x 70½") inner border strips. From navy, cut 2 (2½" x 78½") and 2 (2½" x 74½") outer border strips. Set border strips aside.

For combination strips, cut 2½"-wide crosswise strips (selvage to selvage) as follows: 25 red, 14 navy, and 17 white. Set aside 6 red strips and 10 white strips.

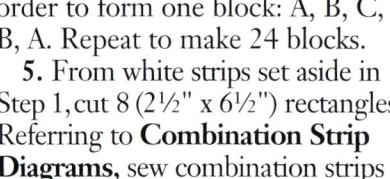
A B C D E
Combination Strip Diagrams

2. Referring to **Combination Strip Diagrams,** sew combination strips as follows:

Combination Strip A (make 3): navy, red, white, red, navy

Combination Strip B (make 3): red, navy, red, navy, red

Combination Strip C (make 2): white, red, navy, red, white

3. Before cutting combination strips, press all seams to the darker side. Cut strips, 2½" wide, across seam lines of combination strips as follows:
48 from Combination Strip A
48 from Combination Strip B
24 from Combination Strip C

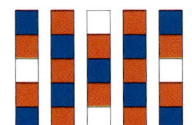 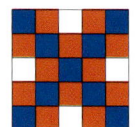
Block Piecing Diagram 1

4. Referring to **Block Piecing Diagram 1,** join 2½"-wide combination strips at sides in following order to form one block: A, B, C, B, A. Repeat to make 24 blocks.

5. From white strips set aside in Step 1, cut 8 (2½" x 6½") rectangles. Referring to **Combination Strip Diagrams,** sew combination strips D and E with a 6½"-wide strip in the center and 2½"-wide strips on sides as follows:

Combination Strip D (make 3): red, white, red

Combination Strip E (make 4): white, white, white

6. Cut 50 (2½"-wide) strips across seam lines of Combination Strip D. Cut 25 (6½"-wide) strips across seam lines of Combination Strip E.

7. Referring to **Block Piecing Diagram 2,** join strips at sides in following order: D, E, D. Repeat to make 25 blocks.

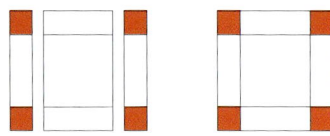
Block Piecing Diagram 2

8. Referring to **Quilt Top Assembly Diagram** for placement, appliqué 1 stem (D), 1 apple (A), and 1 leaf (C) to 1 block. Repeat to make 24 Apple blocks. To remaining block, appliqué 1 stem (D), 1 apple core (B), and 1 leaf (C), referring to **Quilt Top Assembly Diagram** for position of stem and leaf.

9. Join 4 Apple blocks to 3 pieced blocks, beginning with Apple block and alternating Apple blocks and pieced blocks, to make 1 Row 1. Repeat to make 4 Row 1s.

10. Join 3 Apple blocks to 4 pieced blocks, beginning with pieced block and alternating as above, to form 1 Row 2. Repeat to make 3 Row 2s.

11. Join rows, alternating rows 1 and 2.

12. Join 2½" x 70½" green inner borders to sides of quilt. Join 2½" x 74½" green inner borders to top and bottom of quilt, butting corners.

13. Join 2½" x 74½" navy outer borders to sides of quilt. Join 2½" x 78½" navy outer borders to top and bottom of quilt, butting corners.

Quilting
Outline-quilt edges of appliqué. Quilt remainder of quilt with a 1½" cross-hatching pattern.

Finished Edges
Bind with bias binding made from navy fabric.

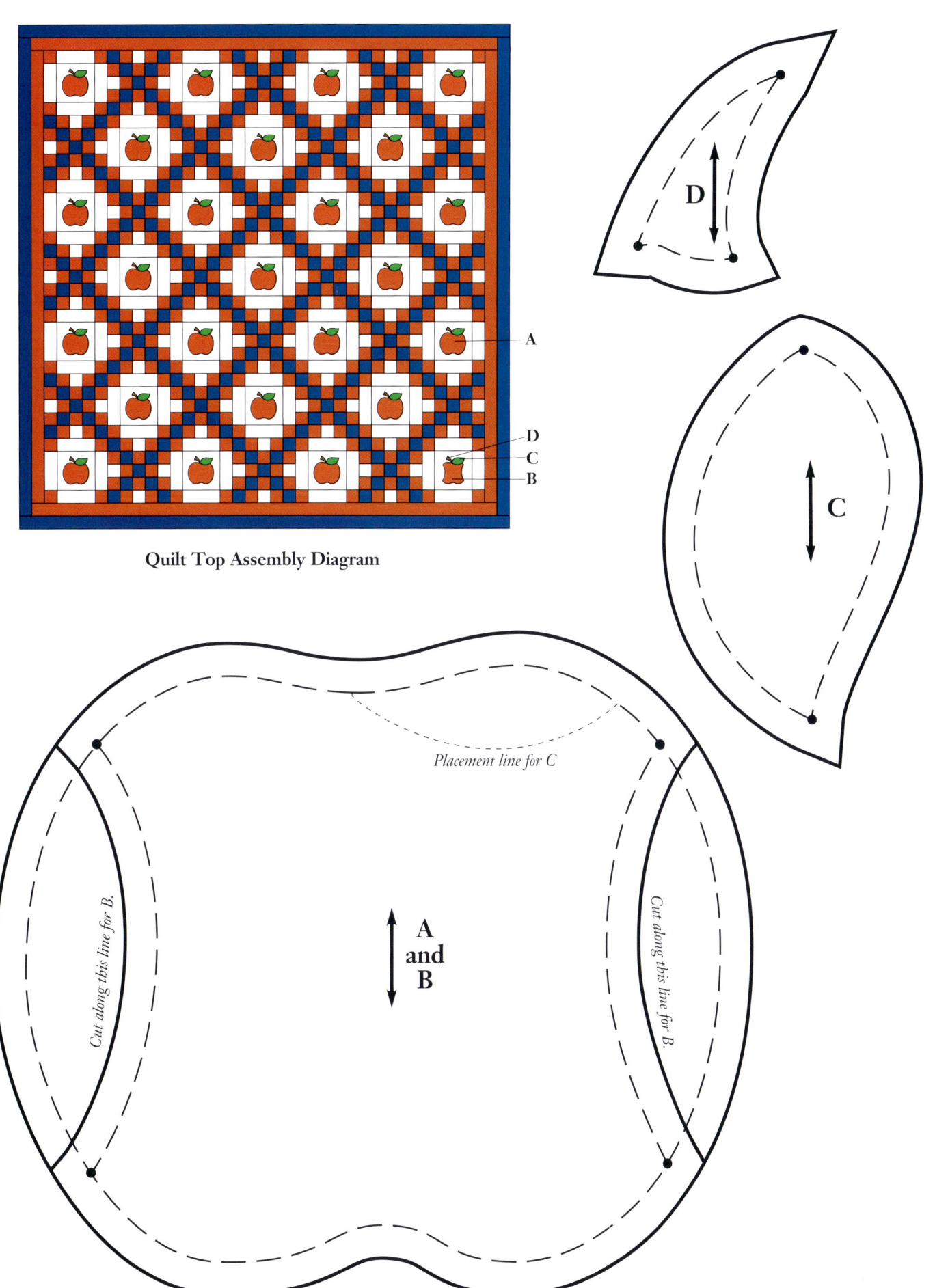

Quilt Top Assembly Diagram

29

Williamsburg Palm

Pauline Spieks made her *Williamsburg Palm* using Hawaiian and freezer-paper appliqué techniques. Its design is similar to a quilt made in 1861 by a woman named Mary Grove; for this reason, it is sometimes known as the Blue Grove quilt pattern.

The blue reminded Pauline of a Williamsburg blue, and the appliqué shape reminded her of a palm leaf—thus the name *Williamsburg Palm*.

Finished Quilt Size
87" x 105"

Number of Blocks and Finished Size
20 blocks   15" x 15"

Fabric Requirements
Blue print*   12¼ yards
Muslin   6½ yards
Backing   9 yards

*Includes fabric for bias binding.

Other Materials
Freezer Paper

Number to Cut
Template A   58 blue print
Template B   4 blue print
Template C   4 blue print

Quilt Top Assembly

1. From muslin, cut 20 (15½") squares. Also from muslin, cut 2 (6½" x 105½") and 2 (6½" x 87½") outer border strips.

From blue print, cut 2 (3½" x 93½") and 2 (3½" x 75½") inner border strips. Also from blue print, cut 4 (3½" x 87½") sashing strips and 16 (3½" x 15½") sashing strips.

Set squares and strips aside.

2. From blue print, cut 20 (19") squares. Fold 1 square in half vertically and horizontally. Place palm leaf template on folded square as shown in **Palm Leaf Placement Diagram.** Cut along curved edges as shown. Unfold fabric and set aside. Repeat to cut 20 palm leaves.

3. Trace the complete palm leaf pattern *without seam allowances* onto the dull side of a 19" square of freezer paper. Cut out pattern. Repeat to make 20 patterns.

4. Center 1 freezer-paper pattern, shiny side up, on the *wrong* side of 1 fabric palm leaf. Pin in place. Turn seam allowance under, clipping where needed to smooth curves, and press to fuse seam allowance to shiny side of freezer paper. Remove pins.

Center palm leaf on muslin square and appliqué. Slit muslin behind appliquéd palm leaf and gently remove freezer paper to complete 1 block.

Repeat to make 20 blocks.

5. Referring to **Setting Diagram,** join 5 blocks with 4 short sashing strips to make 1 vertical row. Repeat to make 4 vertical rows. Join rows with long sashing strips.

6. Join 3½" x 75½" blue print inner borders to top and bottom of quilt. Join 3½" x 93½" blue print borders to sides of quilt, mitering corners.

7. Fold muslin outer borders in half lengthwise and press to form appliqué placement guidelines. Join 6½" x 87½" muslin outer borders to top and bottom of quilt. Join 6½" x 105½" muslin borders to sides of quilt, mitering corners.

8. Prepare cable pieces (A, B, and C) using freezer paper as directed in steps 3 and 4. Referring to **Cable Placement Diagram,** pin pieces to borders. Note placement of pieces so that no raw edges are showing. Appliqué cable pieces. Slit muslin behind each cable piece and gently remove freezer paper.

Quilting
Outline-quilt all appliquéd edges. Quilt sashing strips with ¾" diagonal cross-hatching pattern.

Finished Edges
Bind with bias binding made from blue print.

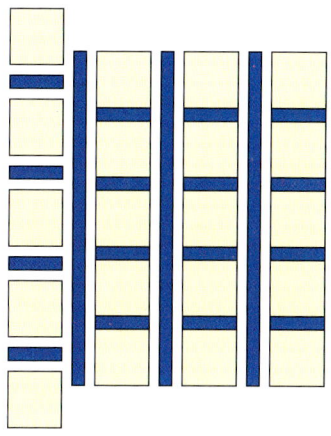

Setting Diagram

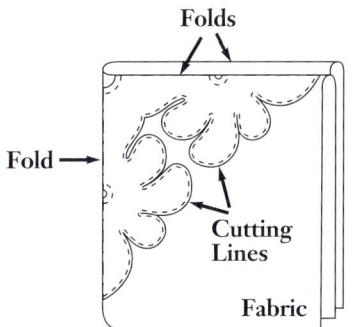

Palm Leaf Placement Diagram

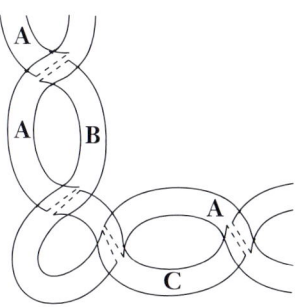

Cable Placement Diagram

Quilt by Pauline Spieks, Stone Mountain, Georgia

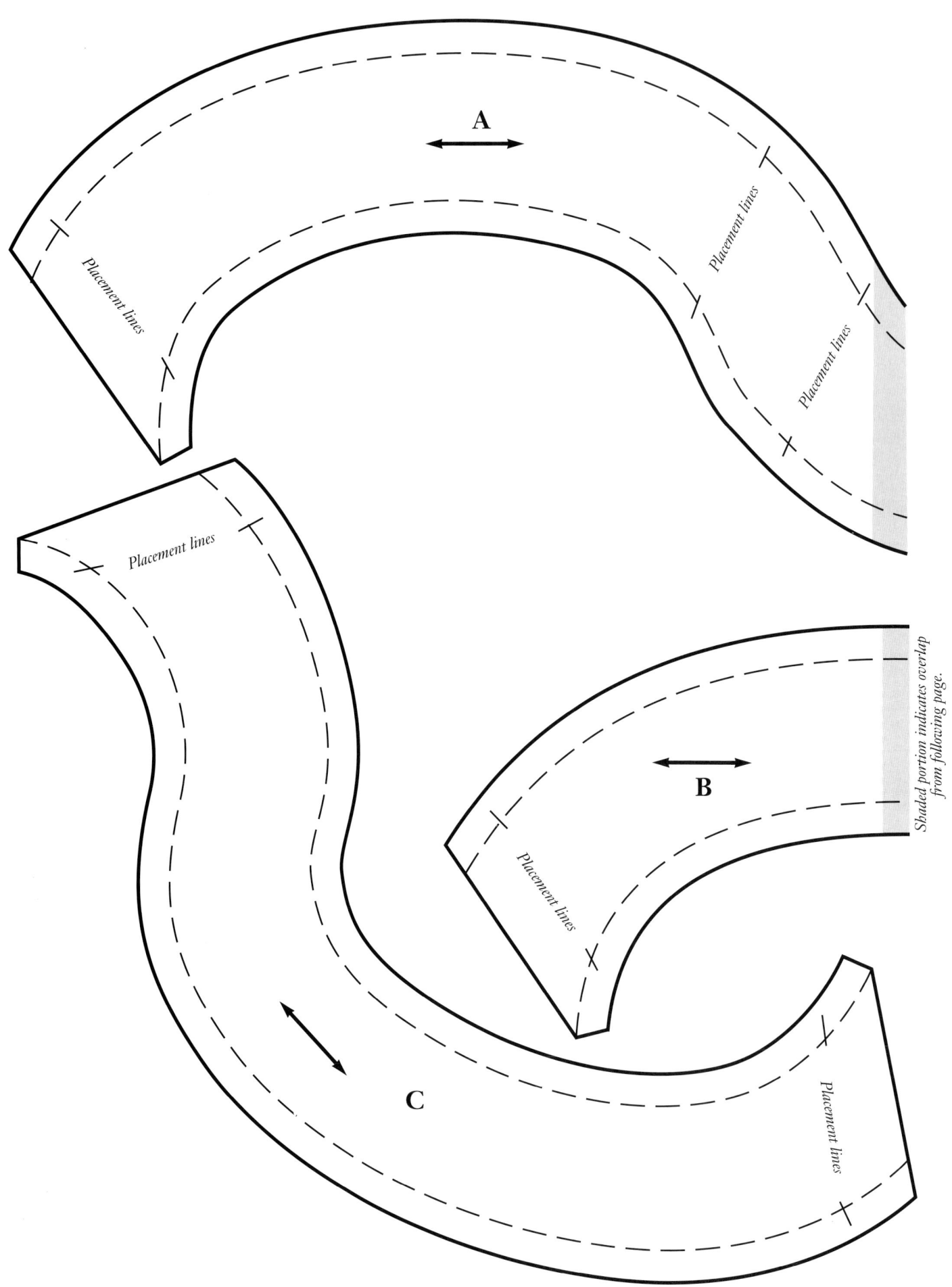

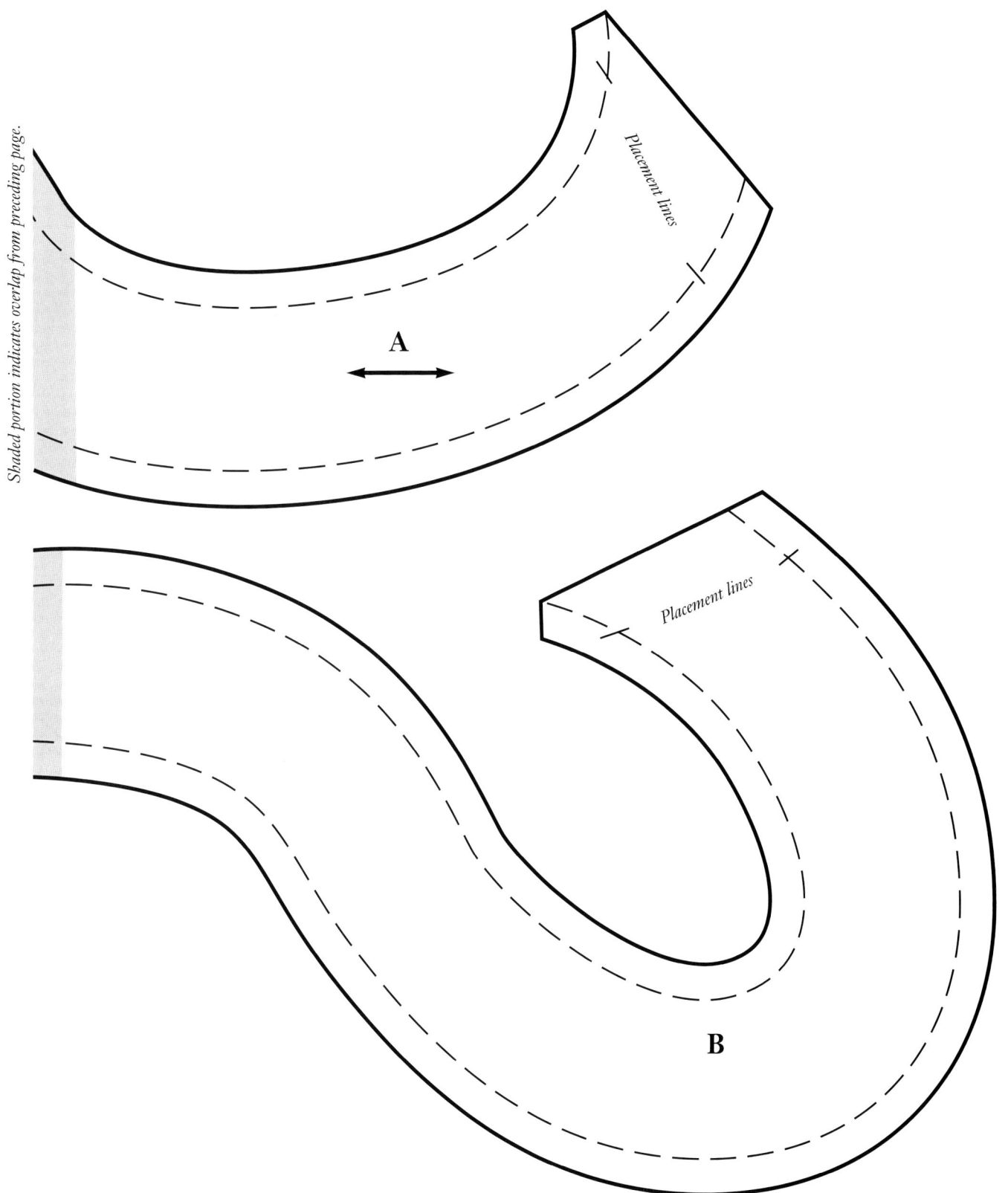

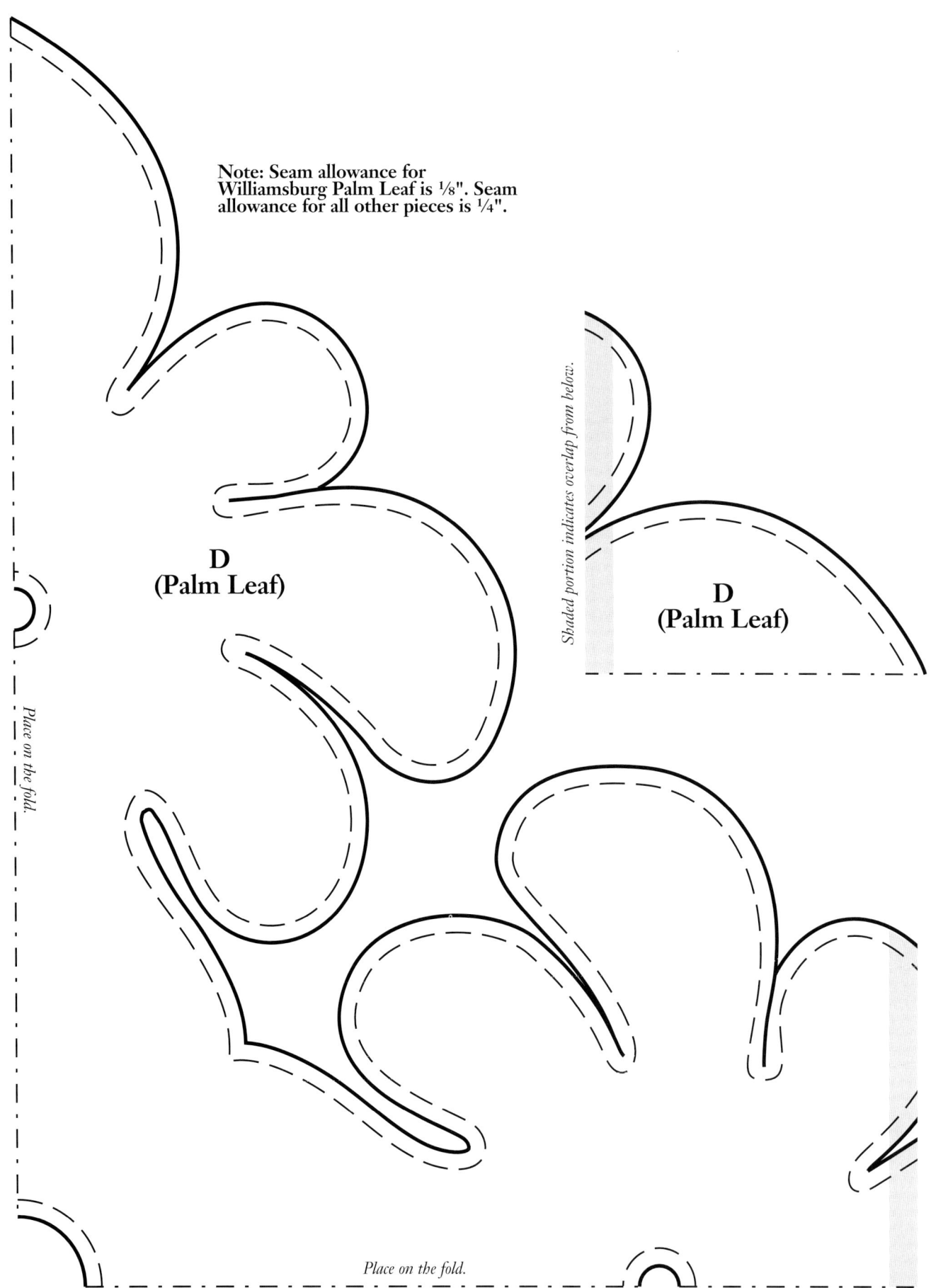

*Quilt by Donna McCulloch,
Klamath Falls, Oregon*

My Daisy

While Donna McCulloch was making a Double Wedding Ring quilt, some of the extra pieces dropped on the floor, and the interesting dispersion of the fabric pieces reminded her of a daisy. So it is easy to see why Donna claimed these daisies as her own.

"*My Daisy* was one of my first tries at creating my own design," says Donna, "and it gave me the courage to try other things on my own."

Finished Quilt Size
89¼" x 107"

Number of Blocks and Finished Size
16 blocks   20" x 24"

Fabric Requirements
White   5½ yards
Yellow   2½ yards
Apple green*   4¼ yards
Dark brown   ¼ yard
Backing   8 yards

*Includes fabric for bias binding.

Other Materials
Lightweight
  fusible interfacing   5¾ yards
Glue stick

Number to Cut
Template A   112 yellow
Template B   32 apple green
Template C   16 dark brown
Template D   16 apple green

Quilt Top Assembly
Note: The following instructions are for machine appliqué. You may use hand appliqué if you prefer.

1. From apple green, cut 2 (2¾" x 87¼") and 2 (2¾" x 107¾") border strips. Set aside.

Also from apple green, cut 24 (2¾" x 21") sashing strips. From yellow, cut 9 (2¾") sashing squares. Set sashing strips and squares aside.

From white, cut 16 (20½" x 24½") background blocks.

2. Prepare daisy pieces (A, B, C, and D) for machine-appliqué by applying lightweight fusible interfacing to each piece. Using glue stick and referring to **Placement Diagram,** anchor pieces to 1 background block. Satin-stitch over raw edges using matching thread to complete 1 daisy block. Repeat to make 16 daisy blocks.

3. To make 1 block row, join 4 daisy blocks with 3 (2¾" x 24½") apple green sashing strips. Repeat to make 4 block rows.

4. To make 1 sashing row, join 4 sashing strips and 3 sashing squares, beginning with a sashing strip. Repeat to make 3 sashing rows.

5. Alternating block rows with sashing rows, join rows.

6. Join 2¾" x 87¼" border strips to top and bottom of quilt. Join 2¾" x 107¾" border strips to sides of quilt, butting corners.

Quilting
Outline-quilt all daisy pieces. Quilt block backgrounds with 1" diagonal cross-hatching pattern, alternating directions for adjacent blocks. Quilt borders as desired.

Finished Edges
Bind with bias binding made from apple green.

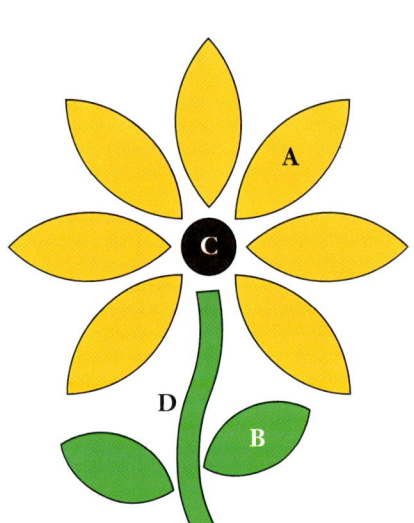

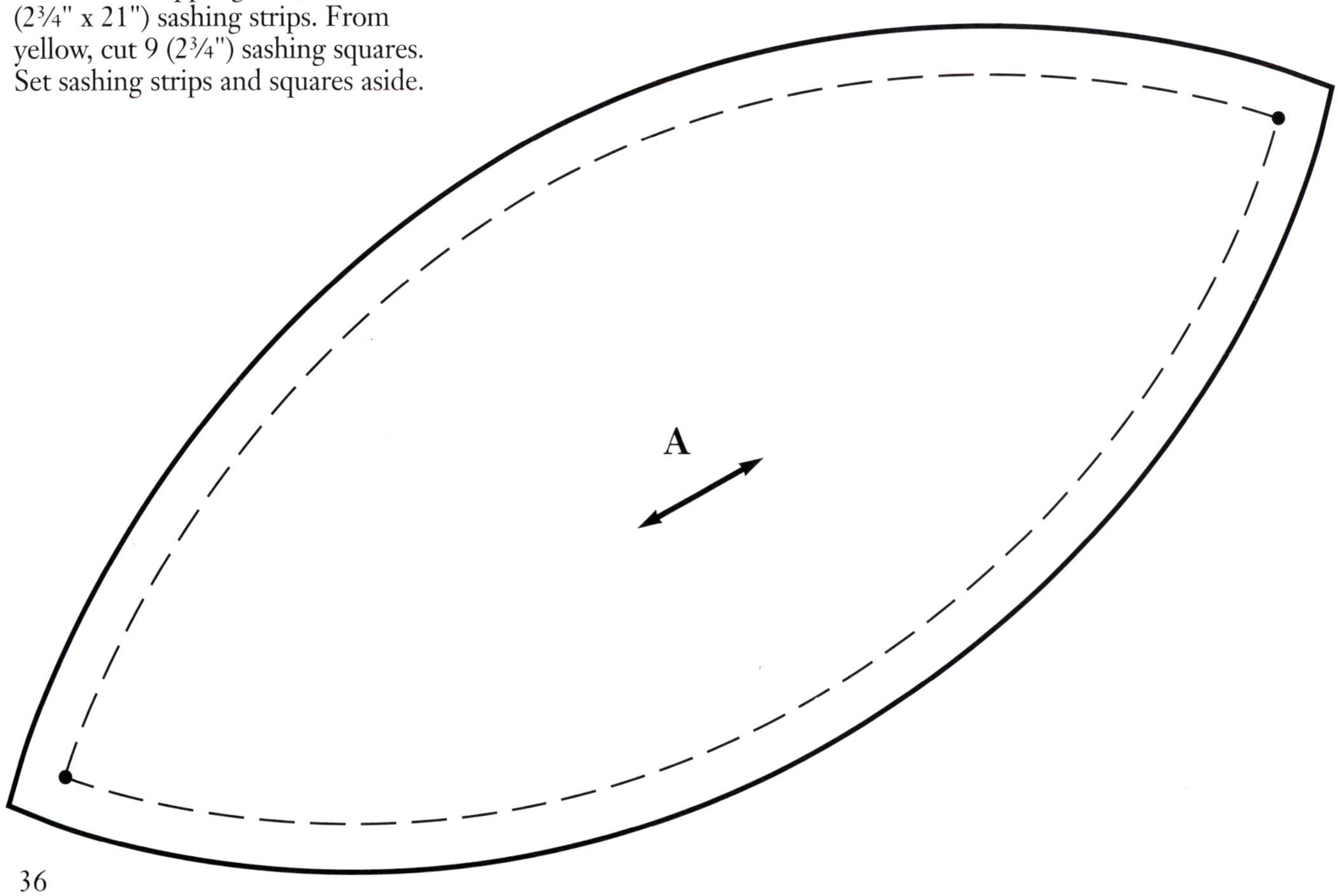

Placement Diagram

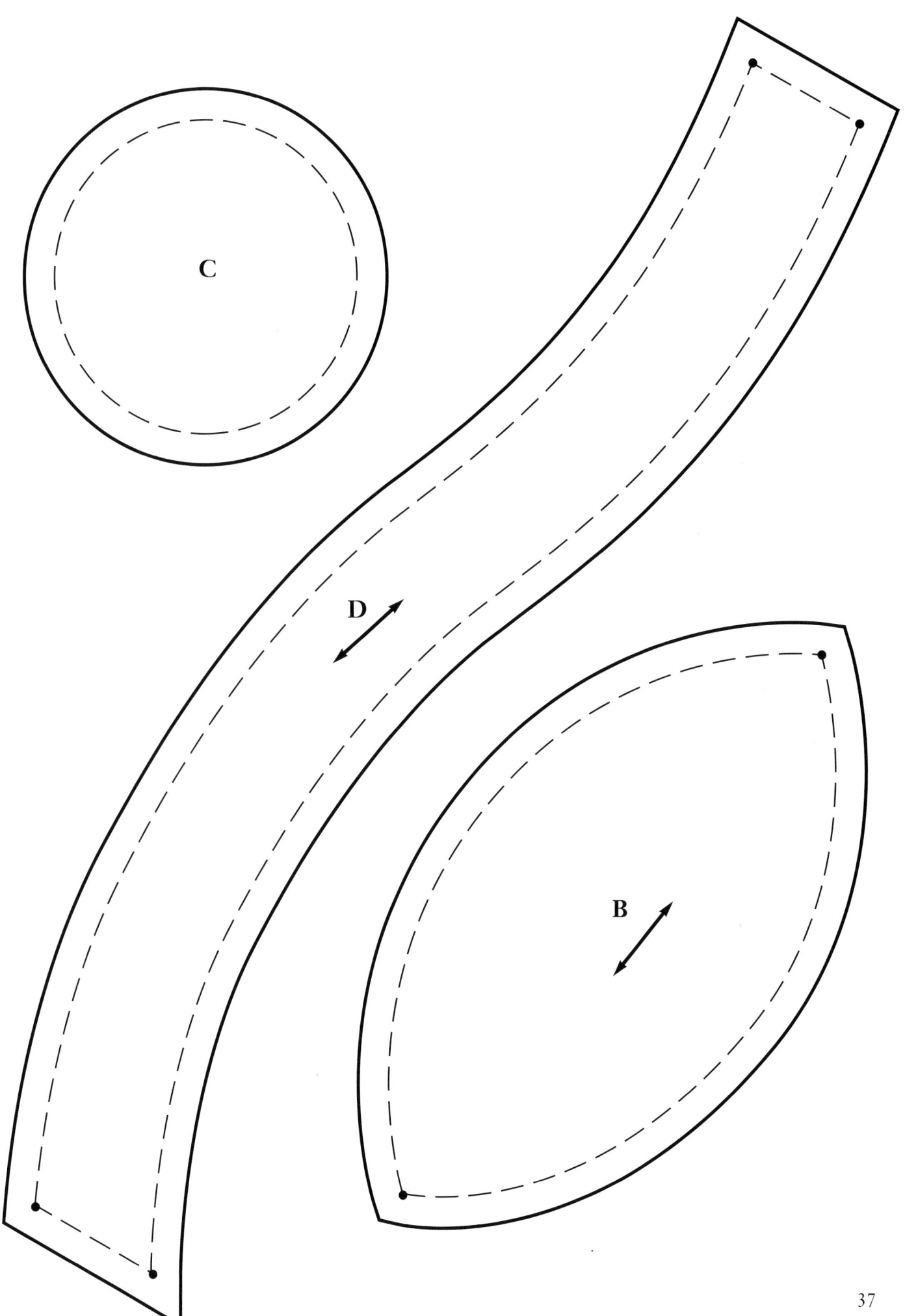

Tulips

*Quilt by Penelope Wortman,
Candler, North Carolina*

When Penelope Wortman first saw a quilt of this design in a photograph, just a small part of it was showing, but she was attracted to it because she had never seen the design before. After finding the pattern, which is a variation of the traditional Crossed Tulips pattern, she adapted the design so that she could complete *Tulips* with lap quilting. Using this technique, she completed the quilting in small, manageable sections and then joined the quilted portions together.

Finished Quilt Size
60" x 76"

Number of Blocks and Finished Size
12 blocks   16" x 16"

Fabric Requirements
White   4 yards
Red print   2½ yards*
Green print   3¾ yards
Backing   4½ yards

*Includes fabric for bias binding.

Number to Cut
Template A   52 red print
Template B   52 green print
Template C   58 red print
Template D   58 green print
Template E   12 red print
Template F   14 green print

Quilt Top Assembly

1. From white, cut 2 (6½" x 64½") and 2 (6½" x 60½") strips for borders. Set aside.

2. Also from white, cut 12 (16½") squares. To mark appliqué guidelines shown on **Placement Diagram,** fold 1 square in half diagonally and finger-press. Unfold square, refold along opposite diagonal, and finger-press. Unfold square, fold square into quarters, and finger-press. Repeat to mark remaining squares.

3. Referring to **Placement Diagram,** arrange 4 As, 4 Bs, 4 Cs, 4 Ds, and 1 E on 1 square, centering pattern pieces on finger-pressed diagonal guidelines. Appliqué pieces to square in alphabetical order to form 1 Tulips block. Repeat to appliqué a total of 12 Tulips blocks.

4. Join blocks in 3 rows of 4 blocks each. Join rows.

5. Join 6½" x 64½" borders to sides of quilt. Join 6½" x 60½" borders to top and bottom of quilt, butting corners.

6. Referring to **Placement Diagram** and quilt photograph, arrange blossoms (A), flowers (B), buds (C), stems (D), and swags (F) on borders. Appliqué (F)s, (C)s, and (D)s to border in that order.

7. To mark corners of scalloped border, use a plate or other round object of desired diameter. Using piece F as a guide for scalloped edge, mark borders between corners. (Trim edges after quilting is completed.)

Quilting
Echo-quilt all blocks and borders as shown in photograph.

Finished Edges
With right sides facing, sew a continuous bias strip of red print to quilt top along lines marked for scallops. Ease bias strip on outside curves and pivot at point on inside curves. Trim all layers of quilt to ¼". Miter or tuck inside curves. Turn binding to back and blind-stitch in place.

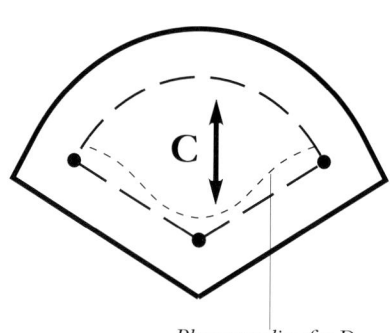

Placement line for D

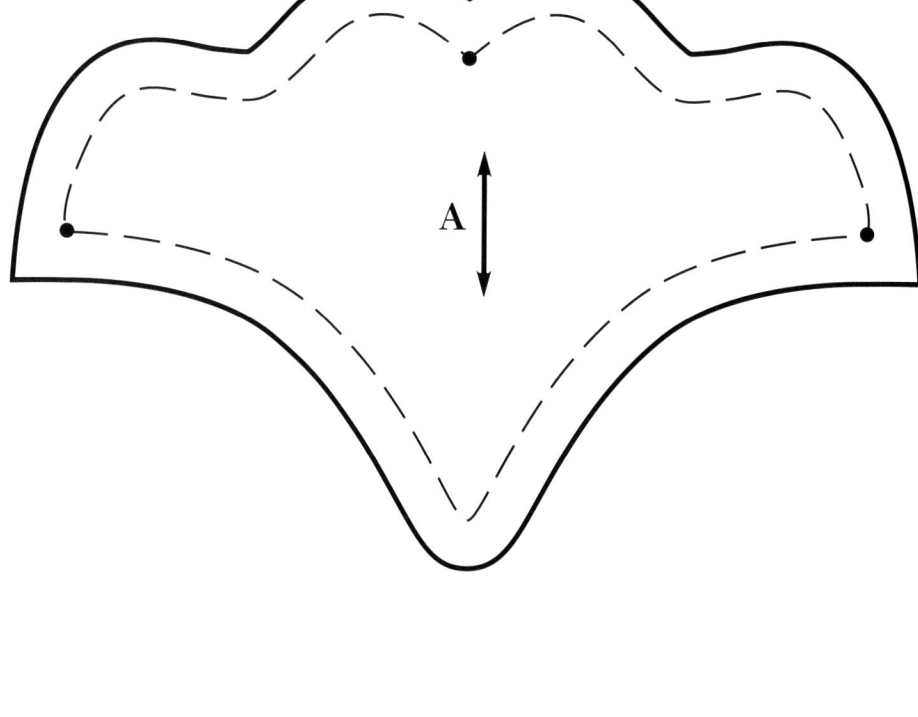

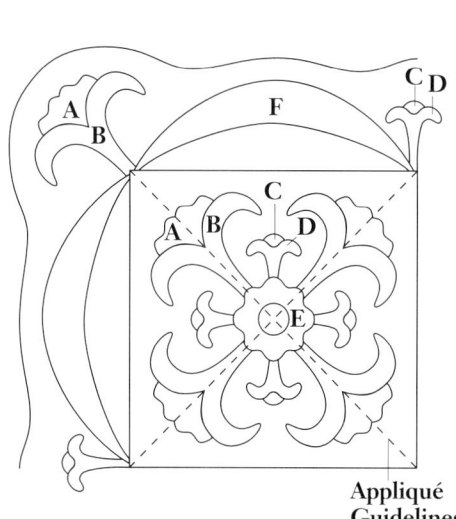

Appliqué Guidelines

Placement Diagram

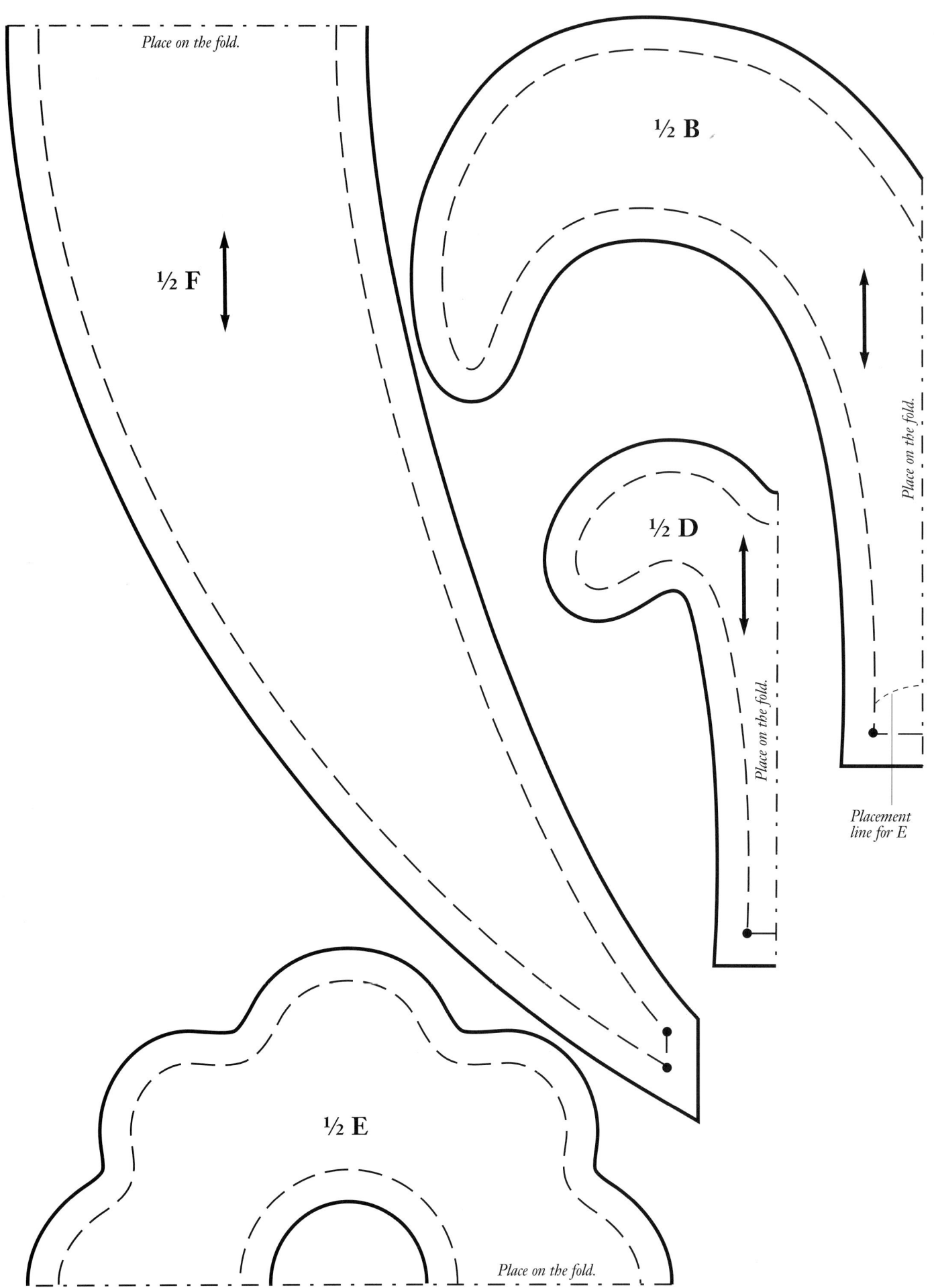

Quilt by *Jana L. Jackson,*
Houston, Texas

Calico Scallops

As a native Floridian, Jana Jackson longed to make a quilt that reminded her of her home state. "My mind conjured up memories of green ocean water, lots and lots of shells, and the whitest sand," says Jana. So she designed her scallop quilt with white to represent the sand, green for the water, and peach for the scallops. She quilted fish and sea horses in the borders and a variety of shells in the setting blocks.

41

Finished Quilt Size
88" x 108"

Number of Blocks and Finished Size
12 blocks   14" x 14"

Fabric Requirements
Peach prints   3 yards total*
White   5⅓ yards
Green print   5½ yards**
Backing   9½ yards

*Use scraps or select ½ yard each of 10 different peach prints.

**For bias strips, borders, and bias binding.

Number to Cut
Template A   12 peach prints
Template A rev.†   12 peach prints
Template B   12 peach prints
Template B rev.†   12 peach prints
Template C   12 peach prints
Template C rev.†   12 peach prints
Template D   12 peach prints
Template D rev.†   12 peach prints
Template E   12 peach prints
Template E rev.†   12 peach prints
Template F   12 peach prints
Template F rev.†   12 peach prints

†Flip or turn over template if fabric design is not reversible.

Quilt Top Assembly

1. From white, cut 18 (14½") squares, 3 (21") squares, and 2 (10¾") squares. Cut 21" squares into quarters diagonally and discard 2 triangles to make 10 setting triangles. Cut 10¾" squares in half diagonally to make 4 corner triangles. Set squares and triangles aside.

2. To make 1 scallop, refer to **Scallop Piecing Diagram 1** and join 1 each of pieces A through F to make a half scallop. Repeat using pieces A rev. through F rev. for other half. Referring to **Scallop Piecing Diagram 2,** join halves. Appliqué scallop to center of 1 (14½") square to complete 1 block. Repeat to make 12 blocks.

3. Referring to **Quilt Top Assembly Diagram,** join scallop blocks, remaining 14½" squares, setting triangles, and corner triangles in diagonal rows. Join rows.

4. From green print, cut 2 (14½" x 88½") and 2 (14½" x 108½") border strips. Join to quilt, mitering corners. (Round corners after quilting is completed.)

5. From green print, cut 14 bias strips, 1" wide. Join ends of strips to form 1 long bias strip. Turn under ¼" on each long raw edge of bias strip and press. Center strip over block seams as shown in photograph and pin in place. Trim excess strip. Appliqué all strips going in one direction first, and then appliqué the ones going in the opposite direction so that overlap will be uniform.

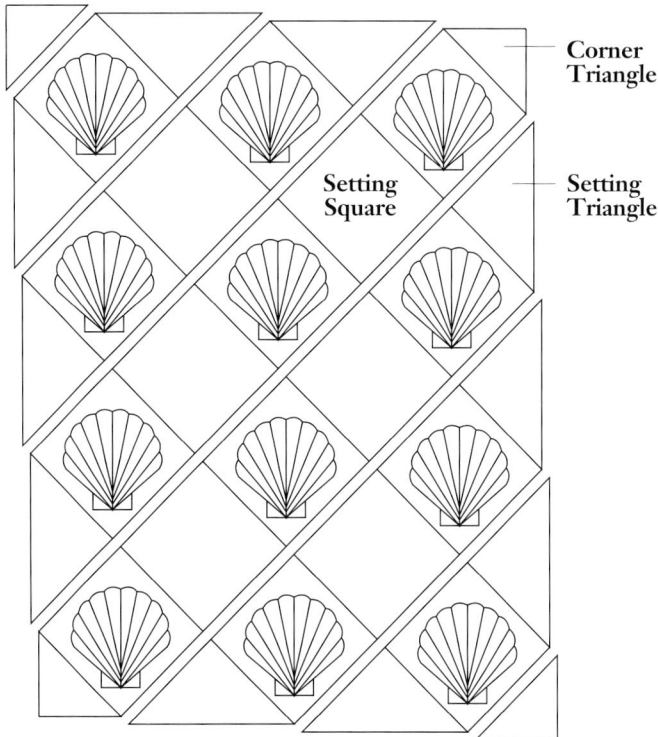

Quilt Top Assembly Diagram

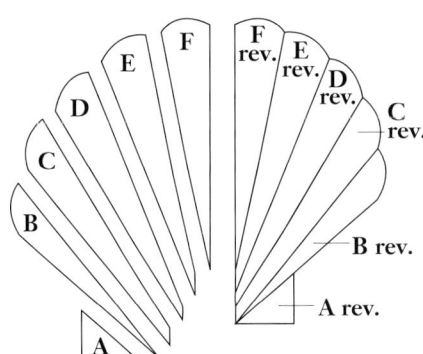

Scallop Piecing Diagram 1

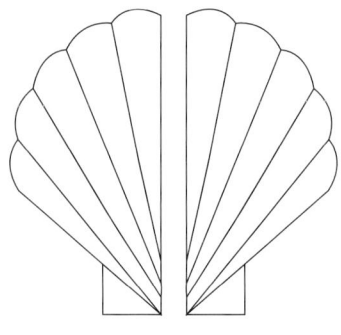

Scallop Piecing Diagram 2

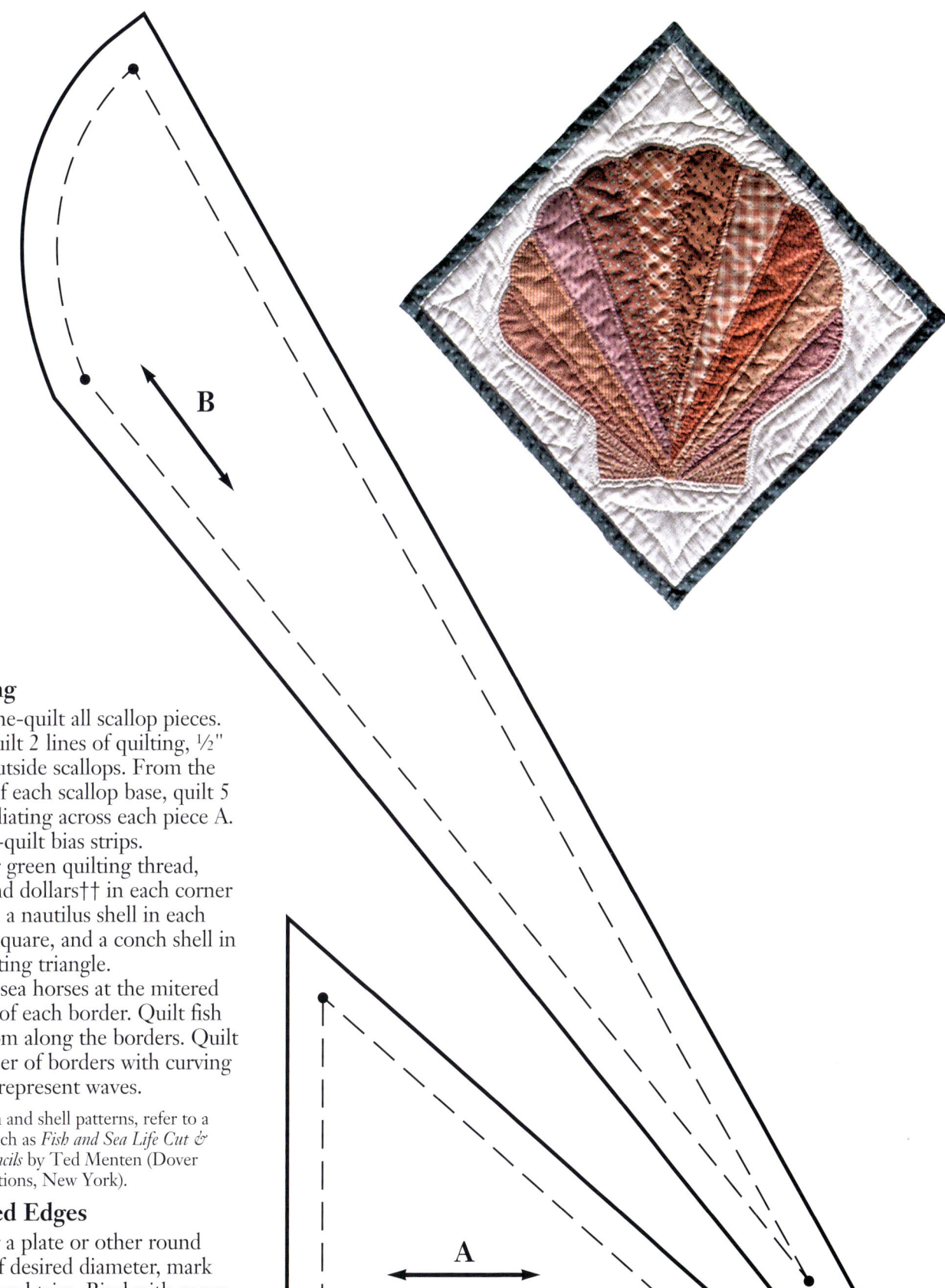

Quilting

Outline-quilt all scallop pieces. Echo-quilt 2 lines of quilting, ½" apart, outside scallops. From the center of each scallop base, quilt 5 lines radiating across each piece A. Outline-quilt bias strips.

Using green quilting thread, quilt sand dollars†† in each corner triangle, a nautilus shell in each setting square, and a conch shell in each setting triangle.

Quilt sea horses at the mitered corners of each border. Quilt fish at random along the borders. Quilt remainder of borders with curving lines to represent waves.

††For fish and shell patterns, refer to a book such as *Fish and Sea Life Cut & Use Stencils* by Ted Menten (Dover Publications, New York).

Finished Edges

Using a plate or other round object of desired diameter, mark corners and trim. Bind with green print fabric.

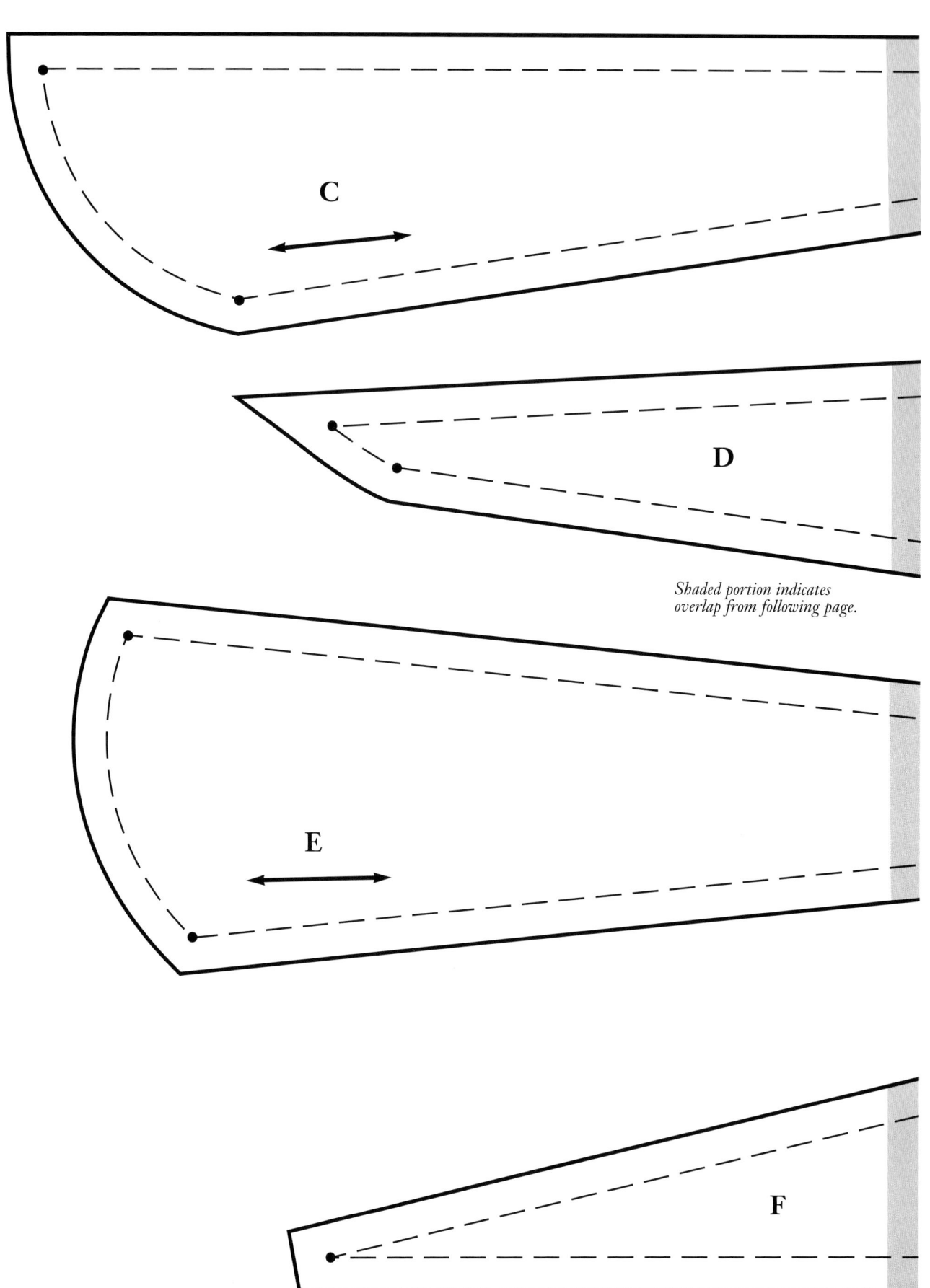

Shaded portion indicates overlap from following page.

Shaded portion indicates overlap from preceding page.

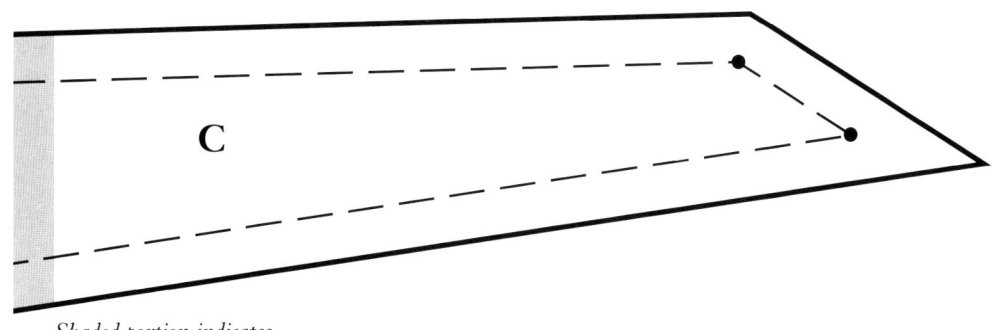

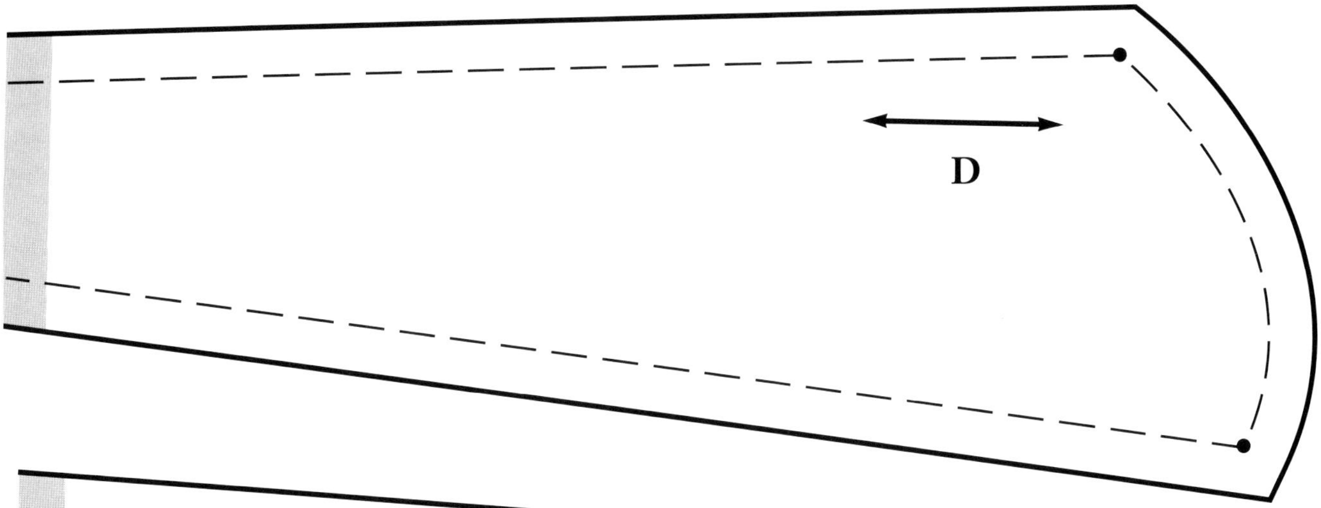

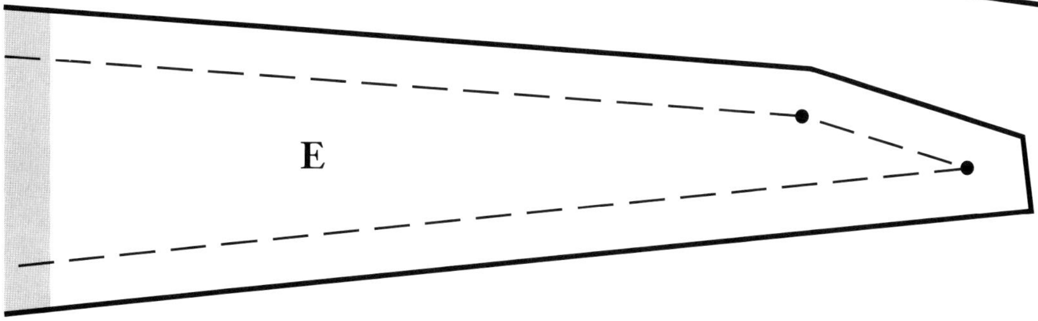

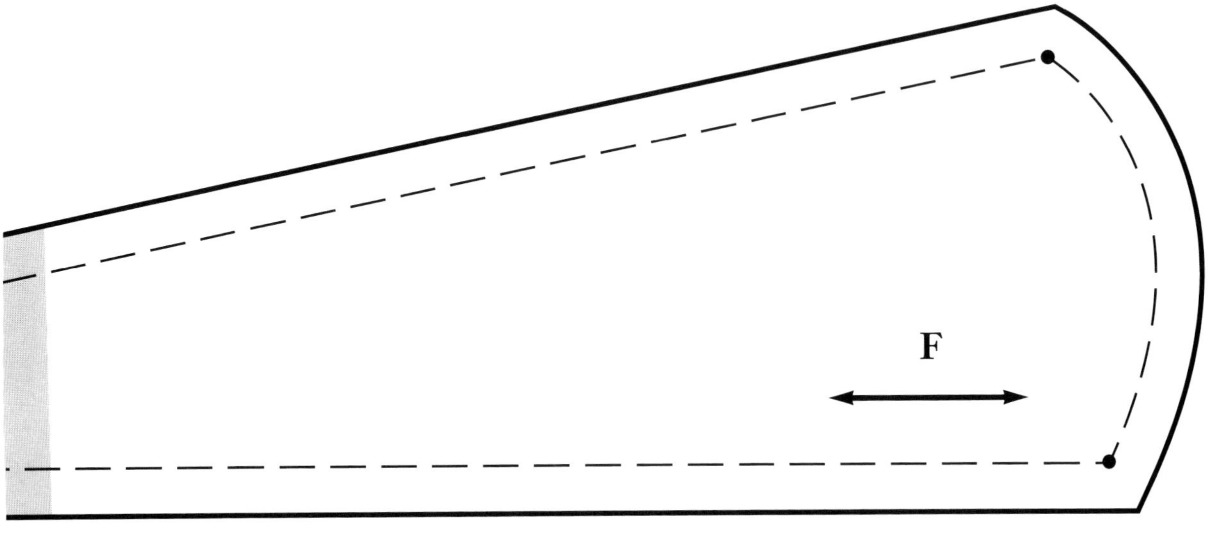

Grapevine

*Quilt by Linda Tinney's Family,
Talladega County, Alabama*

It's not unusual to find a quilt that has been handed down through five generations of the same family. However, it *is* unusual to find a quilt that has been *worked on* by members of those five generations. *Grapevine* was started by Linda Tinney's great-grandmother, Mary E. Powell, who completed one full block and stitched the leaves on the remaining blocks. Linda's grandmother, Sarah Powell Haynes, added the embroidered leaf veins and curling vines. Grace Haynes Johnson, Linda's mother, completed the majority of the exquisite hand quilting. Linda added the grapes and the buttonhole stitching around the leaves. And Karen D. Tinney, Linda's daughter and Mary's great-great-granddaughter, added some of the finishing quilting stitches.

Finished Size
12 blocks 17½" x 17½"

Fabric Requirements
White 5 yards*
Purple 2½ yards
Green 1¾ yards
Backing 5¼ yards

*Includes fabric for bias binding.

Number to Cut**
Template A 144 green
Template B 576 purple

**See Step 1 to cut sashing, borders, and bias stems before cutting other pieces.

Other Materials
Polyester fiberfill stuffing
Green embroidery floss

Quilt Top Assembly

1. From purple, cut 2 (3½" x 80¼") and 2 (3½" x 67½") border strips. Also from purple, cut sashing strips as follows: 9 (1¾" x 18") strips, 4 (1¾" x 74¼") strips, and 2 (1¾" x 58") strips. Set aside.

From green, cut 1 (21") square for bias stems. Following steps 1 through 6 of Continuous Bias Binding instructions on page 11, make a ¾"-wide continuous bias strip. From bias strip, cut 24 (19½"-long) pieces, 48 (5½"-long) pieces, and 144 (1¾"-long) pieces for stems. Fold under ¼" on each long edge of bias strip and press.

From white, cut 2 (2¼" x 76¾") and 2 (2¼" x 61½") border strips. Also from white, cut 12 (18") squares.

2. To mark guidelines for appliqué, fold 1 (18") square in half diagonally and finger-press. Unfold square, refold along opposite diagonal, and finger-press. Repeat to mark all squares.

3. Referring to **Placement Diagram,** arrange 2 (19½") bias stems along diagonal guidelines of 1 square. Arrange 12 (1¾") bias stems and 12 leaves (A) on square as shown. Appliqué stems to square. Appliqué leaves, using buttonhole stitch and 2 strands of green embroidery floss.

For grapes, appliqué 1 grape (B) to square, leaving a small opening along edge. Stuff firmly with polyester fiberfill, using an orange stick or knitting needle to fill grape. Blindstitch opening closed. Appliqué remaining grapes in same manner, referring to **Placement Diagram** for location.

Using 2 strands of green embroidery floss, stemstitch vein accents on leaves as shown on pattern. Outline-stitch grapevine tendrils as shown on **Placement Diagram** to complete 1 block.

Repeat to make 12 blocks.

Continued on next page.

Placement Diagram

47

4. Referring to **Quilt Top Assembly Diagram**, join 3 (1¾" x 18") sashing strips and 4 blocks to form 1 vertical row. Repeat to make 3 rows. Join rows with 2 (1¾" x 74¼") sashing strips. Join remaining 1¾" x 74½" sashing strips to sides of quilt. Join 1¾" x 58" sashing strips to top and bottom of quilt, butting corners.

Join 2¼" x 76¾" white border strips to sides of quilt. Join 2¼" x 61½" white border strips to top and bottom of quilt, butting corners.

Join 3½" x 80¼" purple border strips to sides of quilt. Join 3½" x 67½" purple border strips to top and bottom of quilt, butting corners.

Quilting

Outline-quilt along all appliqué pieces and borders. Quilt blocks in swirl pattern as shown in photograph, or quilt as desired.

Finished Edges

Bind with bias binding made from white fabric.

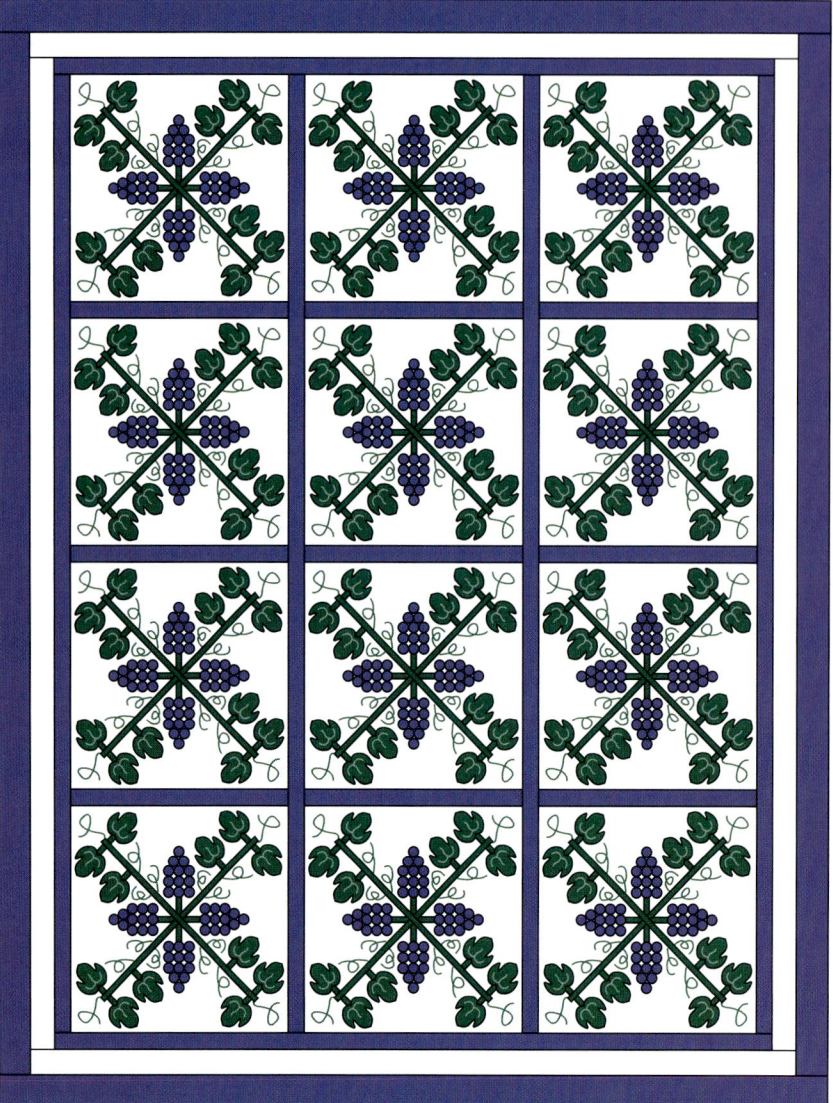

Quilt Top Assembly Diagram

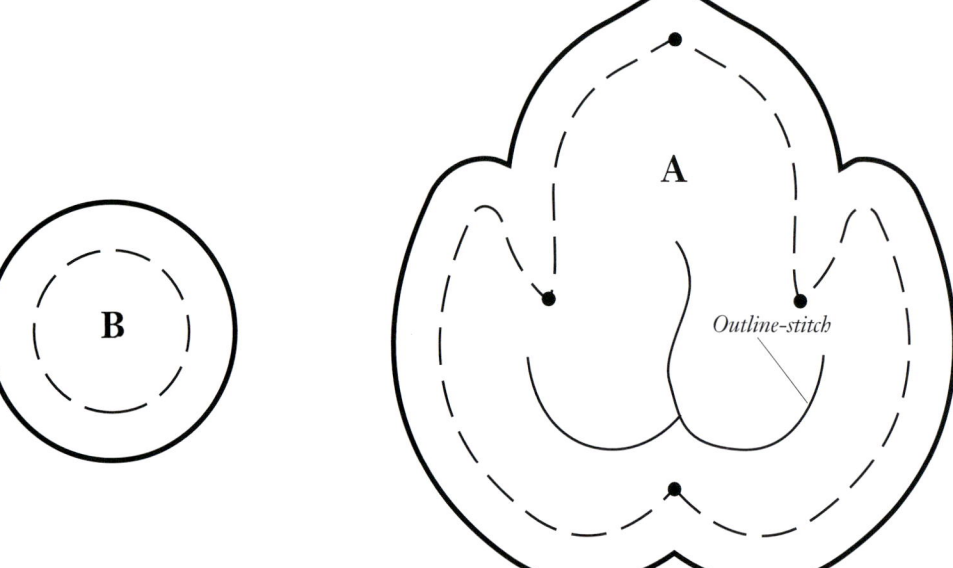

48